BRITISH ARCHITECTURE 1984

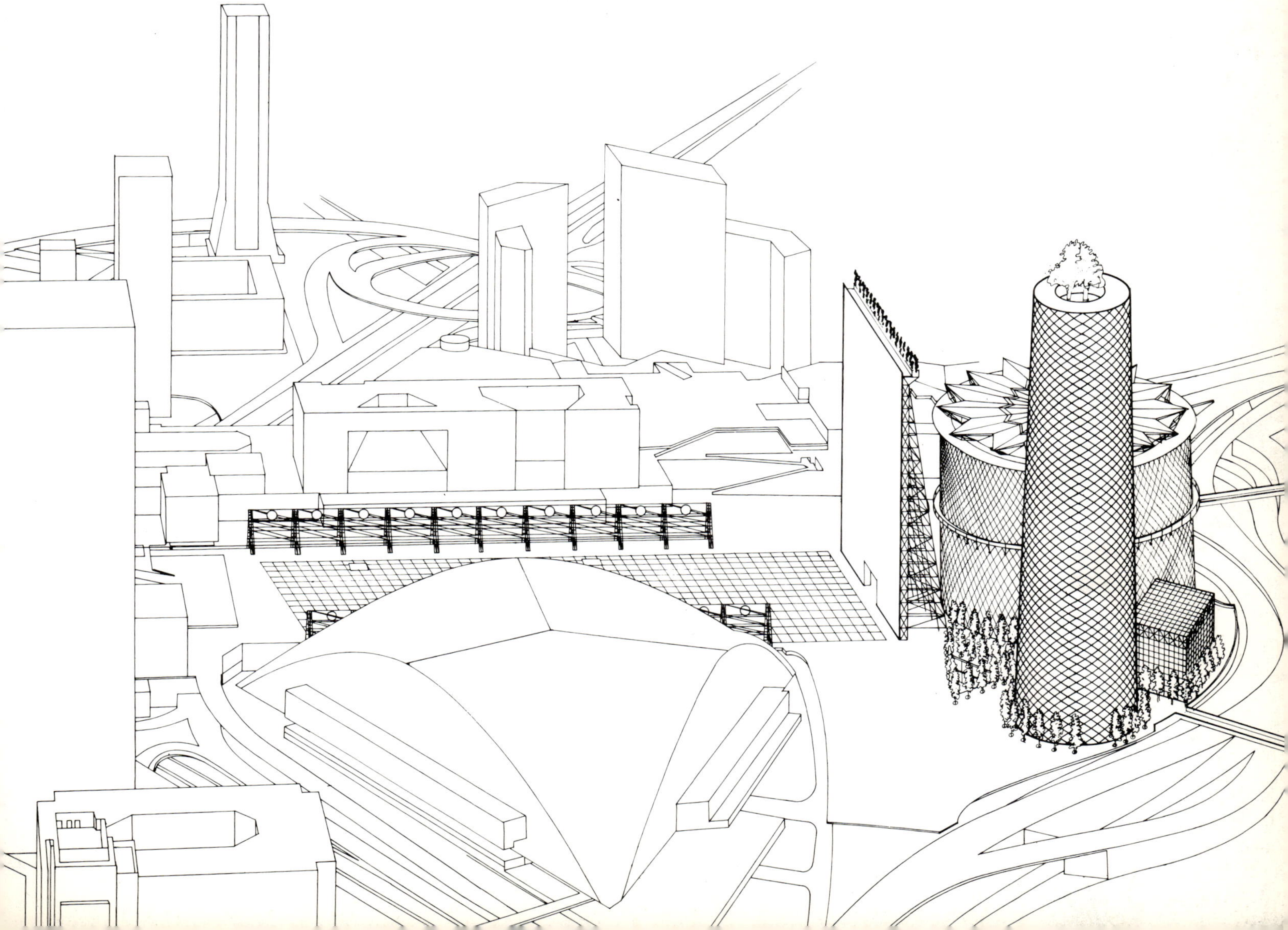

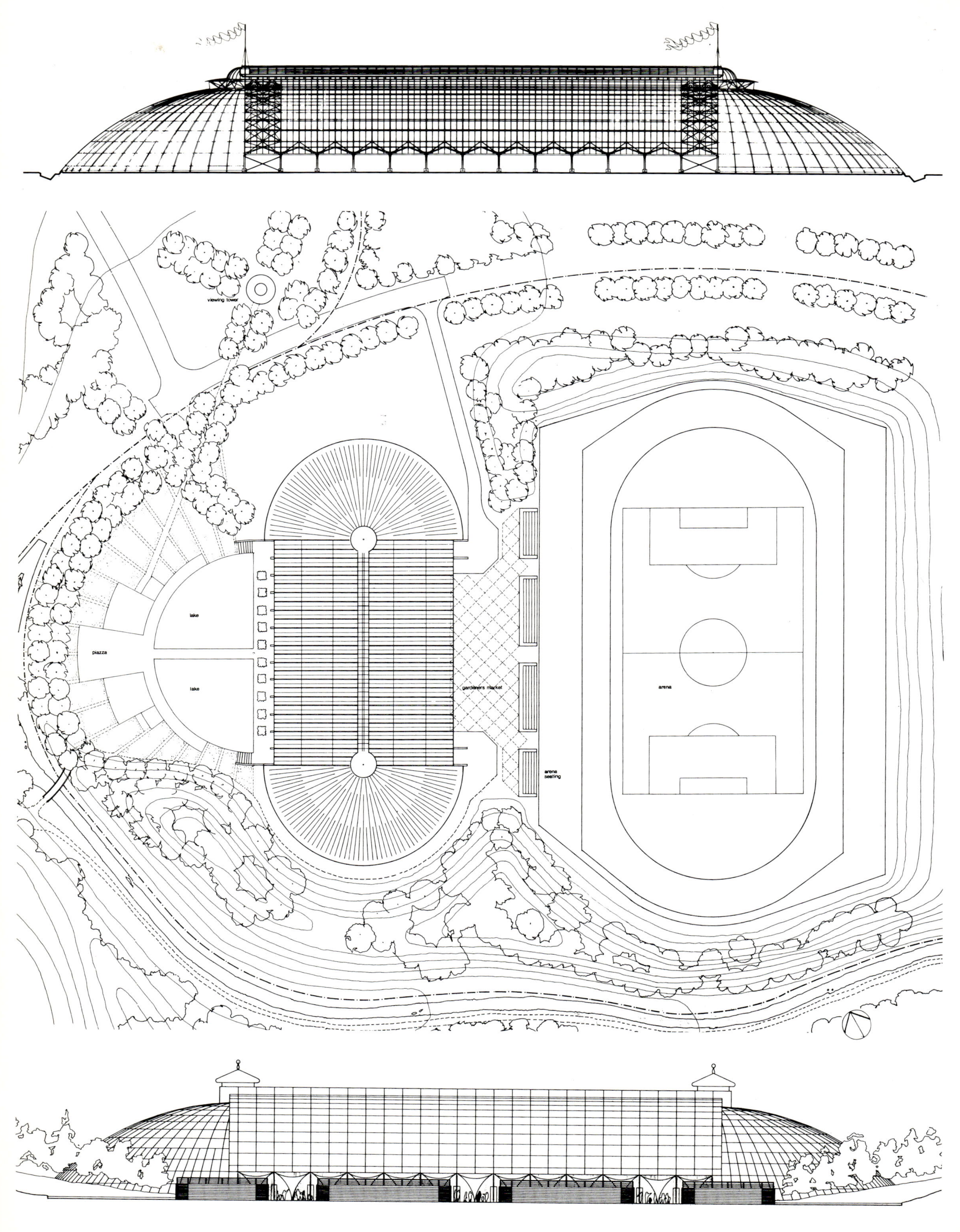
viewing tower
piazza
lake
lake
gardeners market
arena
arena seating

A.D. Architectural Design Profile

BRITISH ARCHITECTURE 1984

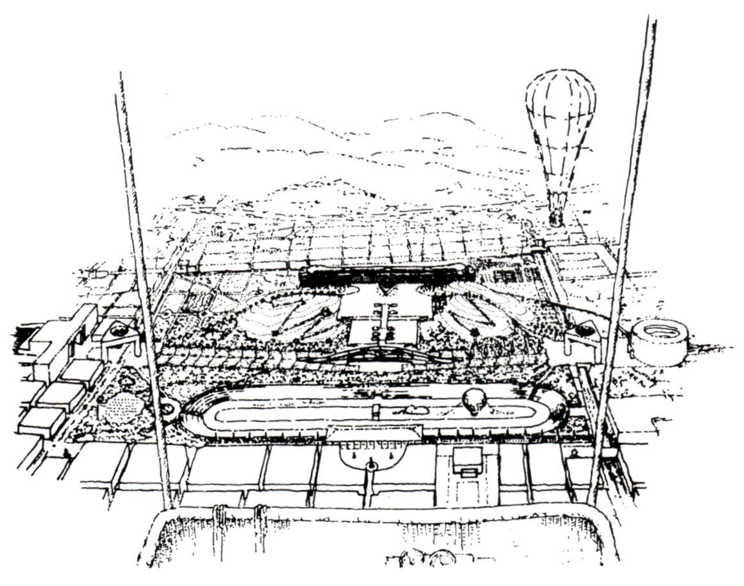

Editor: Dr. Andreas Papadakis

First published in Great Britain in 1984 by Architectural Design
AD Editions, 7 Holland Street, London W8

PAGE ONE: WILL ALSOP, MIKE GOLD & JOHN LYALL, TETE DEFENSE COMPETITION, PARIS.

PAGE TWO: ARUP ASSOCIATES, LIVERPOOL GARDEN FESTIVAL BUILDINGS, 1984.

PAGE THREE: JAMES STIRLING, MICHAEL WILFORD & ASSOCIATES, VILLA LINGOTTO, 1984.

AD Profile 52 is published as part of Architectural Design Volume 54 3/4-1984

Distributed in the United States of America by
St Martin's Press, 175 Fifth Avenue, New York, NY 10010

ISBN 0-85670-845-3 (UK)
ISBN 0-312-10036-1 (USA)

Printed in Great Britain by E.G. Bond Ltd., London

CONTENTS

List of contents in alphabetical order, incorporating all premiations for both 1983 and 1984 Project Awards

ARCHITECTS

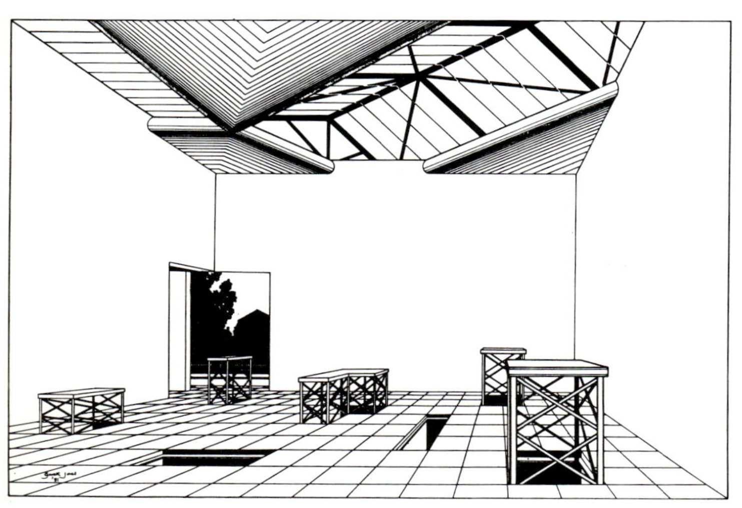

ALSOP, BARNET & LYALL, RIVERSIDE STUDIOS.

ARUP ASSOCIATES, IBM UK LTD, PHASE 4.

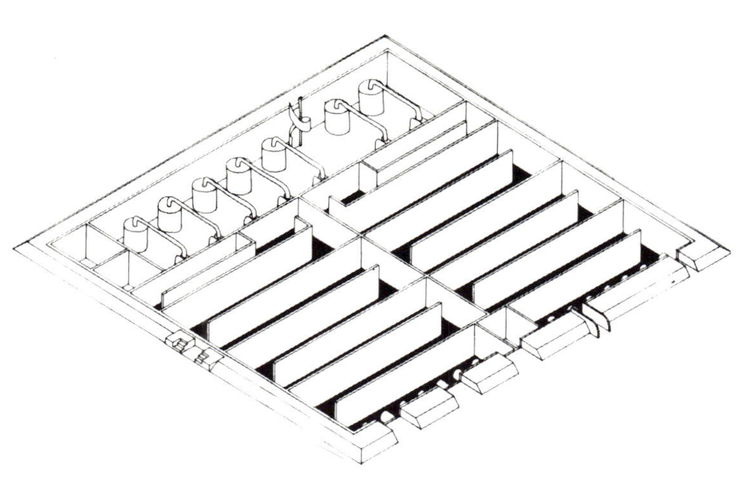

TERRY FARRELL PARTNERSHIP, THAMES WATER AUTHORITY.

NICHOLAS GRIMSHAW & PARTNERS, DIGITAL EQUIPMENT CO.

MICHAEL HOPKINS ARCHITECTS 32
Nursery Industrial Units, Stoke-on-Trent 1983 AWARD (not featured)
Enclosure of Town Square, Basildon, Essex 1983 COMMENDATION
Climatic Research Station, Cambridge 1984 COMMENDATION (not featured)

ROGER HUNTLEY 65
Villas in the People's Park, Belsize Wood 1983 COMMENDATION

EVA JIRICNA 18
Kenzo Shop, Sloane Street, London, 1983 1984 AWARD
Belsize Park Flat, London, 1983 1984 AWARD

JONES & KIRKLAND 10
Mississauga City Hall, 1983 1983 AWARD
Trinity Gardens, Toronto, 1984 AWARD

MACCORMAC JAMIESON & PRICHARD ARCHITECTS 78
Sainsbury Building, Worcester College, Oxford 1984 AWARD
J Sainsbury Supermarket, Canterbury

RICK MATHER ARCHITECTS 80
New Climatic Research Building, University of East Anglia, Norwich, 1985 1984 AWARD

MILTON KEYNES DEVELOPMENT CORPORATION 45
Downhead Park 5 Housing; Bradwell Common Housing; Central Area Infill, Fishermead/Oldbrook, Milton Keynes 1984 COMMENDATION

JOHN MUTLOW (MUTLOW DIMSTER ARCHITECTS) 70
Low Cost Housing Projects, Los Angeles, 1979-82 1983 AWARD

THOMAS NUGENT 13
Interior of Hotel Waiting Area 1984 COMMENDATION

SHEILA O'DONNELL & JOHN TUOMEY 14
House at Ballyweelin, County Sligo, Ireland 1984 AWARD

IAN RITCHIE ARCHITECTS 35
Eagle Rock House, Sussex, 1982 1983 AWARD

RICHARD ROGERS + PARTNERS 88
Whittington Avenue, City of London, 1982-3

COLIN ST JOHN WILSON & PARTNERS 36
The City Polytechnic, Hong Kong

JAMES STIRLING, MICHAEL WILFORD & ASSOCIATES 86
Villa Lingotto, Turin

DEREK WALKER ASSOCIATES 50
Story Village

JULYAN WICKHAM ARCHITECTS 40
Restaurant, wine bar and wine shop, Corney & Barrow, London 1984 COMMENDATION

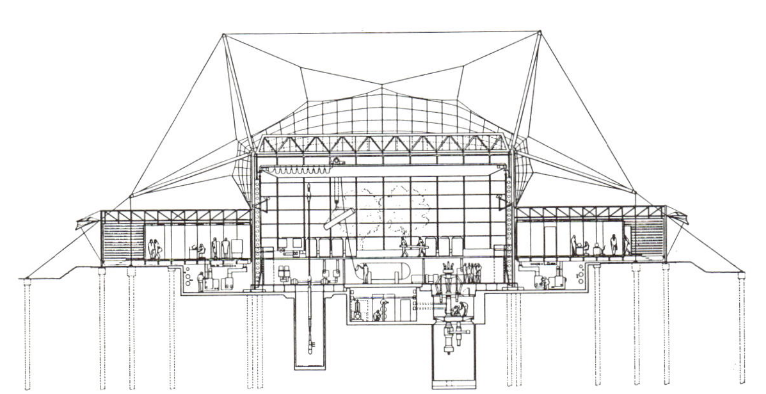

MICHAEL HOPKINS ARCHITECTS, CLIMATIC RESEARCH STATION.

MACCORMAC JAMIESON & PRICHARD, SAINSBURY BUILDING. (PH MARTIN CHARLES)

COLIN LEISK, NICK SUSLAK, JEWELLER'S SHOP.

TASEER, LIBRARY, NOTTING HILL GATE.

STUDENTS

(No student projects are featured)

SIMON BARKER BARTLETT
Schinkenchiku entry 1983 AWARD

NIC BEWICK CANTERBURY
Digital Equipment Co, Reading 1983 AWARD

ROSS CAHILL-O'BRIEN HULL SCHOOL OF ARCHITECTURE
Clydeside Museum, Glasgow 1984 AWARD

J R CARPENTER ARCHITECTURAL ASSOCIATION
Hotel, Gribben Head 1984 AWARD

RUSS DAVENPORT & BILL TAYLOR SHEFFIELD
Fantasia Entertainment Centre, Isle of Dogs 1983 AWARD

THOMAS ELIAS KARAVIS POLYTECHNIC OF CENTRAL LONDON
Kaisariani University Campus, Athens 1984 AWARD

WILLIAM FIREBRACE ARCHITECTURAL ASSOCIATION
Column-Columnist 1983 AWARD

DI HOPE ROYAL COLLEGE OF ART
Swiss Cottage Villas; 7×7×7m House 1983 AWARD

COLIN LEISK, NICK SUSLAK LIVERPOOL
Jeweller's Shop 1983 AWARD

WILLIAM FIREBRACE, COLUMN-COLUMNIST.

SIMON BARKER, SCHINKENCHIKU ENTRY.

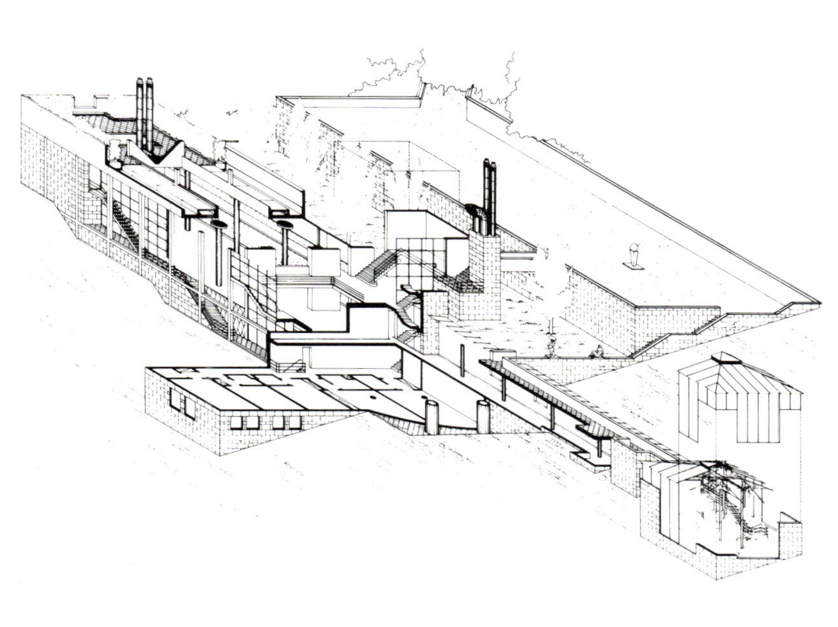

J R CARPENTER, HOTEL, GRIBBEN HEAD.

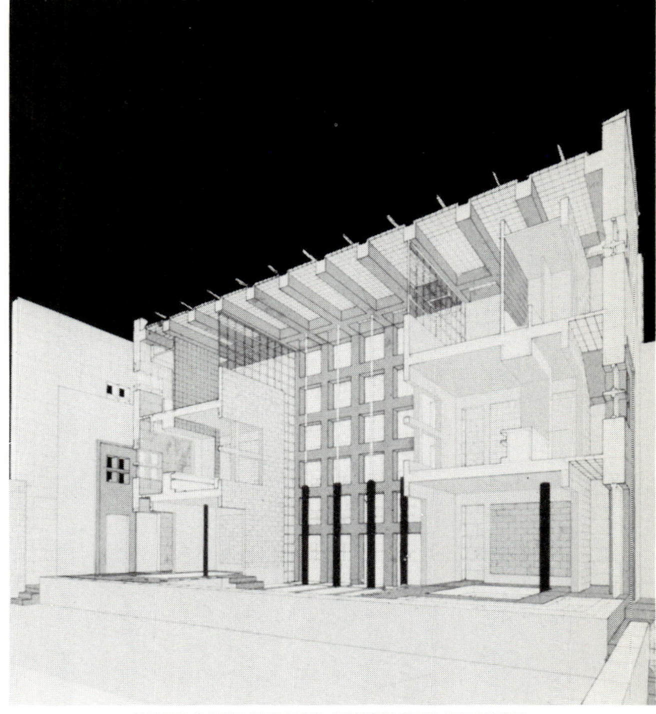

NAVID QAIM-MAQUAMI, CONTEMPORARY HOUSE.

COLIN LEISK, NICK SUSLAK & DAVE KING LIVERPOOL
Kew Gardens Museum 1983 AWARD

RONNIE MURNING POLYTECHNIC OF CENTRAL LONDON
Academy of Music & Public Garden, Coram's Fields, Bloomsbury 1984 AWARD

CHRIS PERKINS POLYTECHNIC OF CENTRAL LONDON
Seventh Heaven Competition, Regent's Park 1984 AWARD

DUANE PHILLIPS ARCHITECTURAL ASSOCIATION
Pedestrian Crossing at the River Thames 1983 AWARD

NAVID QAIM-MAQAMI ARCHITECTURAL ASSOCIATION
Contemporary House 1983 AWARD

IAN R SIMPSON
Maplin In-Town Terminal 1983 AWARD

PETER STEWART POLYTECHNIC OF CENTRAL LONDON
Pliny's Villa 1983 AWARD

HIN TAN LIVERPOOL
House generated by a particular structural form 1983 AWARD

TASEER ROYAL COLLEGE OF ART
Library, Notting Hill Gate 1983 AWARD

STEPHEN TSANG ARCHITECTURAL ASSOCIATION Hotel Acantilado 1984 AWARD

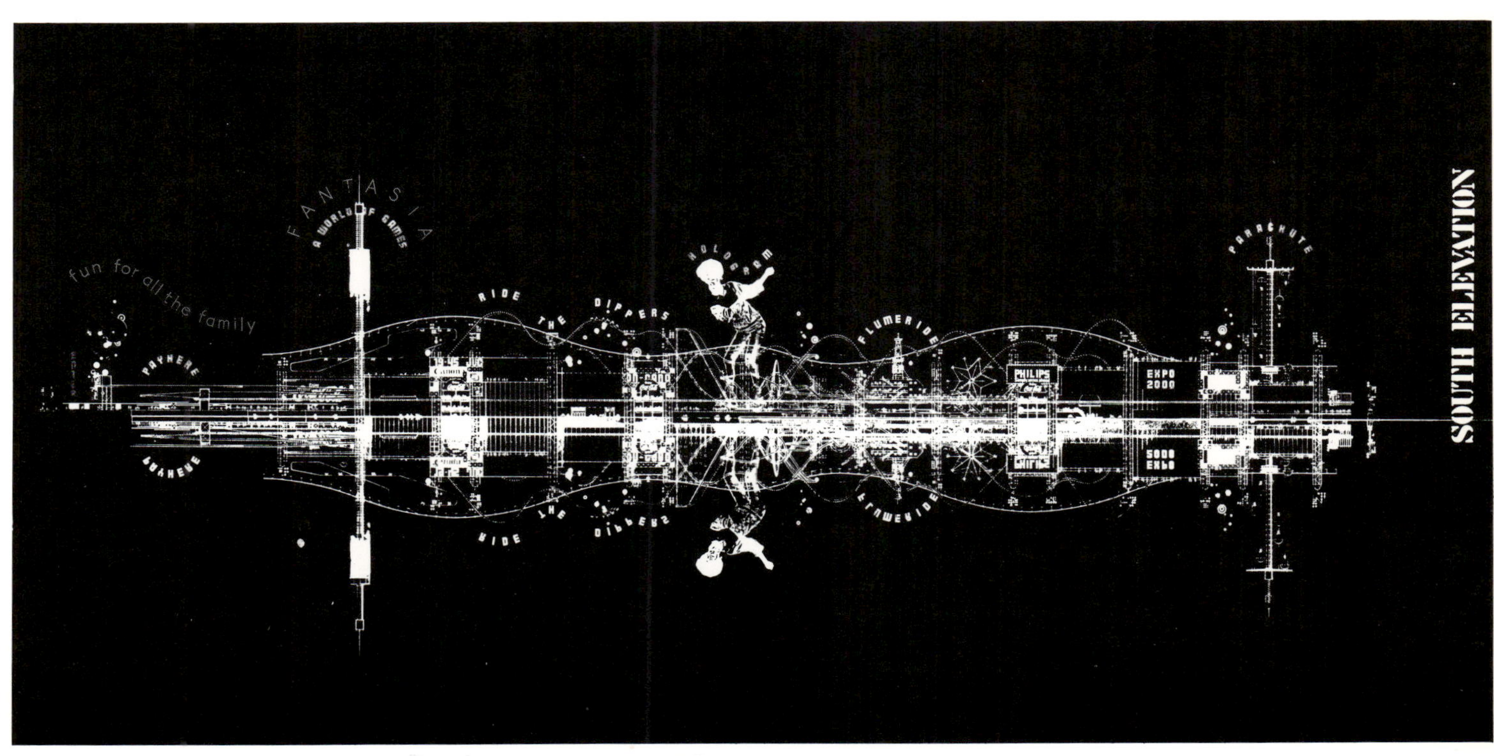

RUSS DAVENPORT & BILL TAYLOR, FANTASIA ENTERTAINMENT CENTRE, ISLE OF DOGS.

CODA LIMITED

Oriental Museum Project, Durham University 1983

1984 AWARD

1 GENERAL PERSPECTIVE.

This project was begun in response to an open competition announced in September 1982, and was one of six projects developed further in a second stage. The requirement for a new exhibition gallery was prompted largely by the failure on all counts of the current gallery building. A product of 1960s University expansion, it is characteristically banal in appearance, inadequate in both physical and spatial performance, and situated with regard to both the steeply graded woodland site and the Victorian classroom building in a manner best described as haphazard. The brief naturally identified an opportunity at this time to link the need for new facilities with a general re-assessment of the building and its use.

The accommodation consists of permanent exhibition area (ground floor) with entrance foyer and flexible changing exhibition area (first floor). A tea-room and an administrative office are housed in a separate 'pavilion' on the site.

In considering the establishment of some pervading value for this ensemble of buildings, the inherent capacity of the site to provide a heightened tension between building and nature offered a strong initial directive. Predictable external views from the periphery of the site, the incidental movement through implicit spaces across the site, and the deliberate movement through the internal enclosures together suggested a repertoire of possible relationships in which the experience of the natural terrain, vegetation and aspect could be enhanced. This variety of scale and degree, evidenced in movement and use, was then contrasted with the powerful primary element of the east-facing concrete wall together with its steel 'double'. Set back from the corner, the walls present a new 'face' to the surrounding campus and valley, while exposing the slope and depth of the site. This quality is augmented by the location of the small teahouse building along the foreground edge of the site. The main exhibition areas shelter from direct light and scrutiny behind these walls, and in both surface and volume are in a continuing contrast with its presence. The varied nature of this contrast is developed further in the articulation of the building fabric, and the choice and refinement of material detail can be consistently measured against that of the nearby concrete wall. The implicit referencing to this wall continues beyond to the surrounding woodland site, with an emphatic sensuous contrast to the external 'corten' cladding.

Such a contrast is also evident in the treatment of the horizontal surfaces, between the illuminated glass floor of the upper exhibition area, the meshed steel decking of the ramp and 'loggia', and the crushed gravel 'hoggin' which finishes the lower floor and surrounding surface to the woodland. Finally, the entrance through these walls and the preferred passage through the building via the loggia offer new perceptions of the immediate surroundings, and reaffirm the primary order of the walls prior to each re-entry into the internal volumes of the upper level changing exhibition gallery.

The project has been guided by a continuing appeal to the sensuous and decidedly physical nature of architecture: an architecture whose presence is measured by 'what it is' rather than 'what it means'. The balance struck between moments of emphasis and quiet must begin with the direct pleasures of constructional depiction. The physical and mechanical logics of building imply a clear identification of elements whose relative value must be carefully and explicitly measured. This sensibility may also be demonstrated at broader scales of endeavour, and so allow disparate issues such as orientation and constructional detail, historical awareness and programmatic hierarchy to develop consistent and harmonious roles.

ARCHITECTS CODA Limited
DESIGN TEAM Peter Salter, Chris Macdonald and Ingrid Morris
STRUCTURAL ENGINEERS Ove Arup and Partners, David Tomlinson, Adrian Faulkner
SERVICE ENGINEERS Max Fordham and Partners, Keith Hanson
QUANTITY SURVEYORS: Davis Belfield and Everest, H F Tunbridge

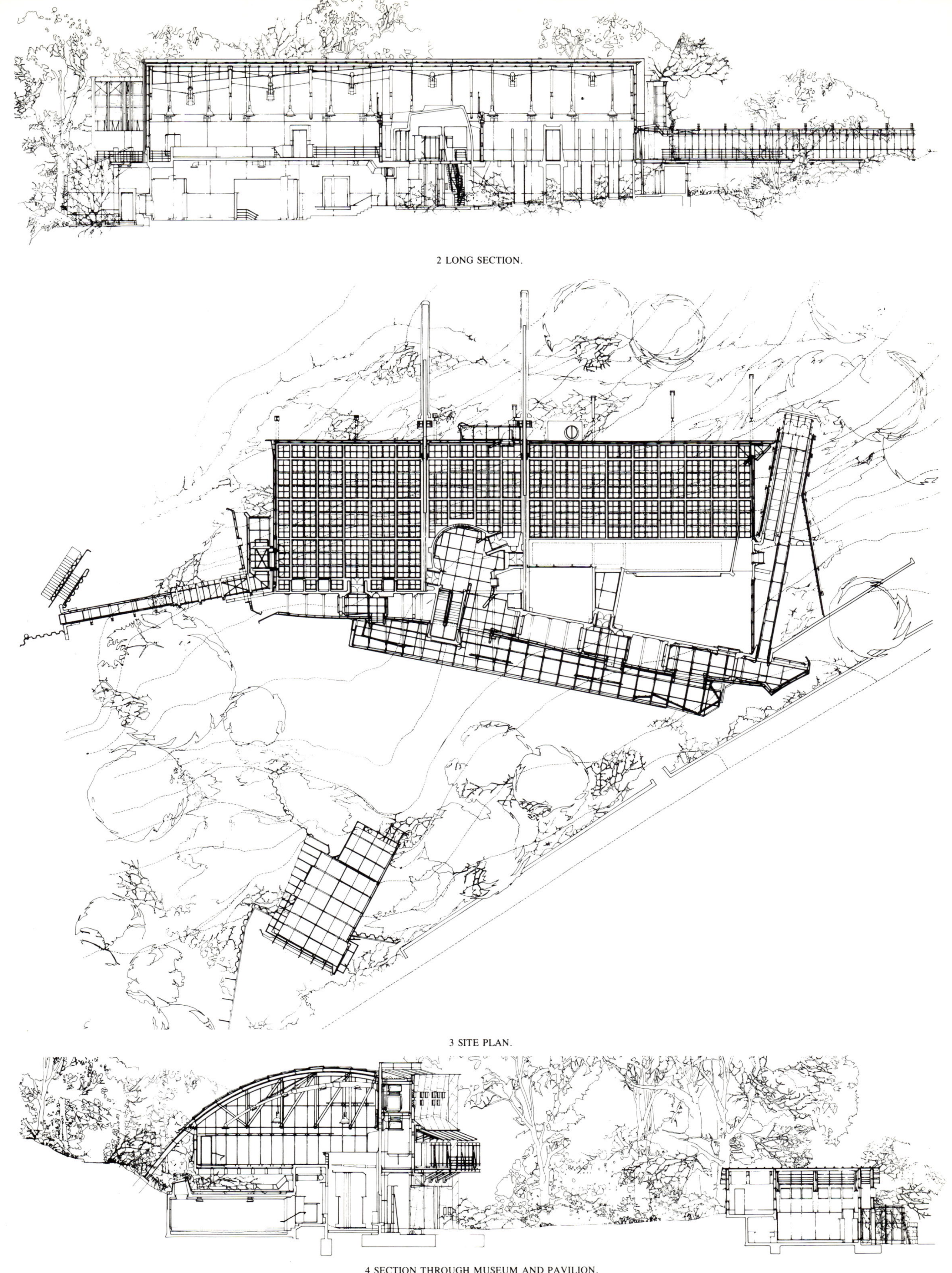

2 LONG SECTION.

3 SITE PLAN.

4 SECTION THROUGH MUSEUM AND PAVILION.

JONES & KIRKLAND
Trinity Gardens, Toronto

1984 AWARD

1 THE SERPENTINE.

Categories of Civic Space
The plan underlines what our proposal is *not* by a comparison with what exists (or what is proposed by the City of Toronto) and as a result we hope to clarify what it is. If we understand Nathan Phillips Square to be a square and St. James Park to be a park, then the residual space around Trinity Church is certainly neither a square nor a park. Its more modest dimensions and its situation within the interior of the urban block characterise it as a garden. In opposition to the commerical bustle of Eaton's arcade, the civic Agora of Nathan Phillips Square and the day of parades down University Avenue, Trinity Gardens suggests itself as a quiet and somewhat remote enclave. As the connection from Bay to Yonge Streets is a major pedestrian route, we propose that it should be distinct and separate from the Gardens.

The Use of Toronto Precedents
There is an impressive range of horticultural types in Toronto capable of withstanding the harsh winters and at the same time affording shade and cool in the summer. The following examples come to mind: the rows of poplars at Fort York and at Central Tech on Bathurst Street; the pleached Chinese elms on Centre Island; the creeper at Canada Maltings; and the existence of privet hedges almost everywhere. (The best example of hedges is in Lawrence Park, run by the City of Toronto). The Winter Gardens and Palm House in Allan Gardens, with their permanent luxuriance and exotic flora, complement the more hardy outdoor species.

Our intention is to amalgamate these familiar Toronto garden elements. We believe their capacity to withstand a harsh geographical climate makes them suitable to withstand the social rigours of a public space.

A Sequence of External Rooms
Our proposal seeks to reverse the contemporary tendency for civic spaces to be ill-defined and vacuous. To this end we propose Trinity Gardens as a series of external 'rooms'. The central garden can be viewed as the grand 'salon', the pergola as its long gallery and the circular garden its rotunda or entrance hall. The illusion to rooms is confirmed by an architectural code: hedge and trellis as wall; pergola and tree canopy as ceiling; lawn as floor or carpet. The 'green house', of course, makes a more literal enclosure.

There are two spatial sequences. Firstly, the principal visual axis, which runs north-south via the ramps from Trinity Church to the rotunda and is bisected by a minor east axis from James Street. The connections are clear although, in the words of Capability Brown, 'the feet may not follow the path the eye has travelled'. Secondly, there is a more secret and leisurely promenade connecting all the secondary spaces beginning from Trinity Church, continuing along the pergola, descending into the serpentine maze with the head of the visitor disappearing unexpectedly into the verdure, continuing through to the Palm House and returning via the two garden rooms back to Trinity Church. At each stage the visitor is able to relate visually back to the central garden.

The Definition and Boundaries of the Site
The garden rooms have been organised so that the overwhelming presence of the existing buildings on the site is reduced.

1 The regular lines of poplar trees encloses Trinity Church and creates a triangular space, reducing the impact of Bay Street and making the entrance to the Eaton Centre by the device of a traditional vista. Looking west from the church door, the form of the space also acts as a 'trompe l'oeil'.

2 The central garden is excavated to 5 feet below existing grade which produces a clear internal focus while the retaining walls reinforce the sense of enclosure.

3 The wall of poplars defining the central garden acts as a visual 'shelter belt' reinforcing the autonomy of the space.

4 The vine canopy to the pergola cuts out the visual dominance of the eighteen-storey Bell Canada building immediately adjacent.

5 The small garden rooms with their canopy of trees and high walls reduce the impact of the back of the Eaton Centre to the east.

The Theme of an Architectural Garden
North American city buildings, despite their solid appearance, have tended to have a transitory nature

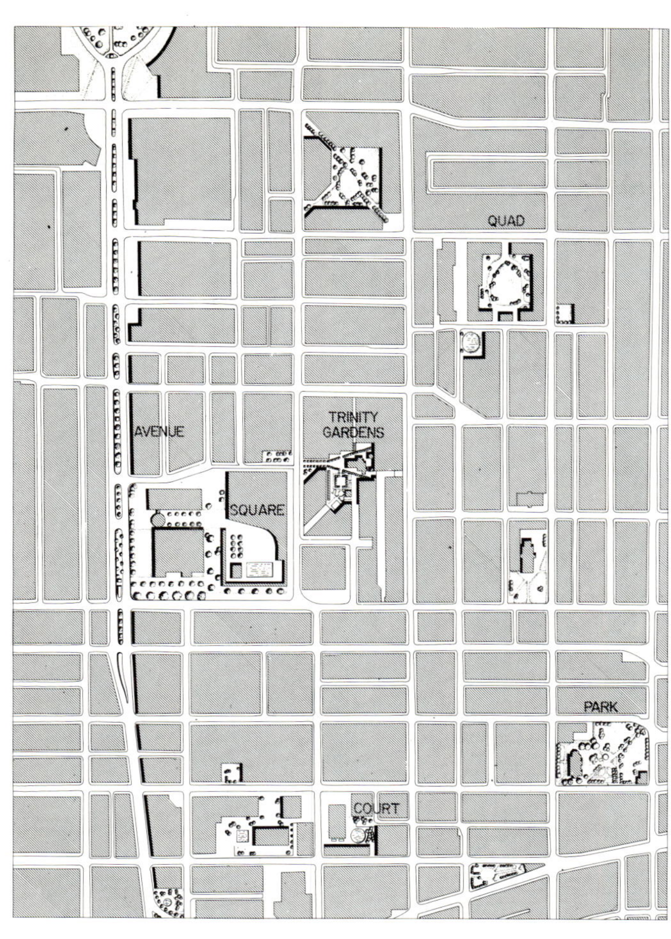

2 CATEGORIES OF CIVIC SPACE, DOWNTOWN TORONTO.

HOTEL
DEPARTMENT STORE
BAY STREET
BELL CANADA
EATON CENTRE
YONGE STREET
SHOPPING ARCADE
OLD CITY HALL
0m 10m 25m 50m 100m

3 AREA PLAN.

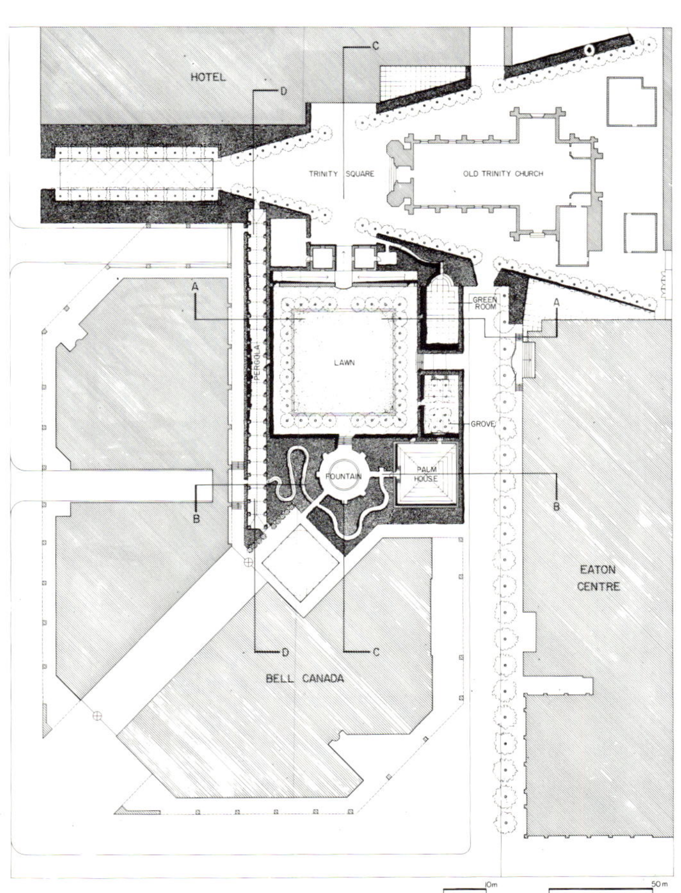

4 SITE PLAN.

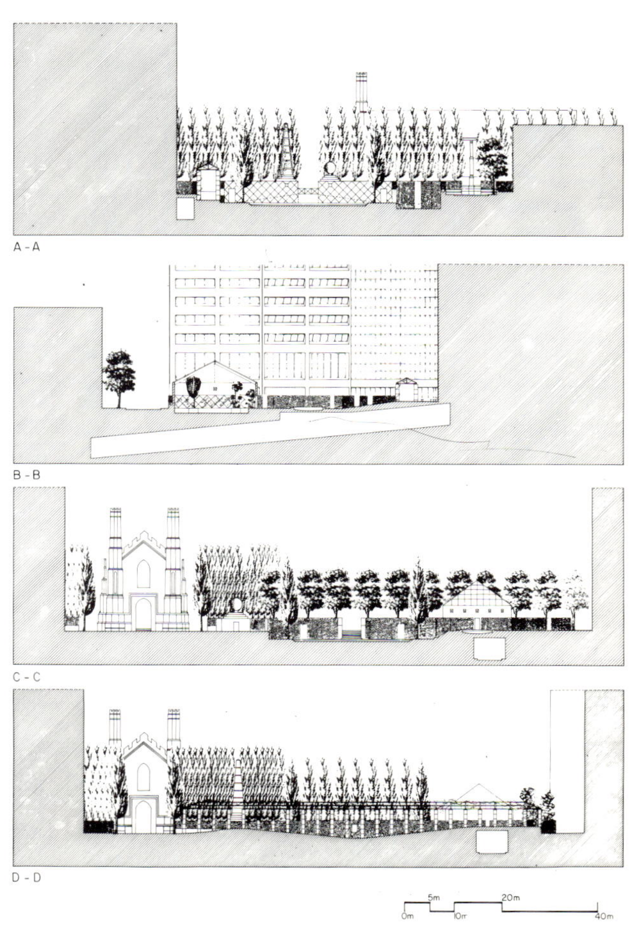

5 SITE SECTIONS.

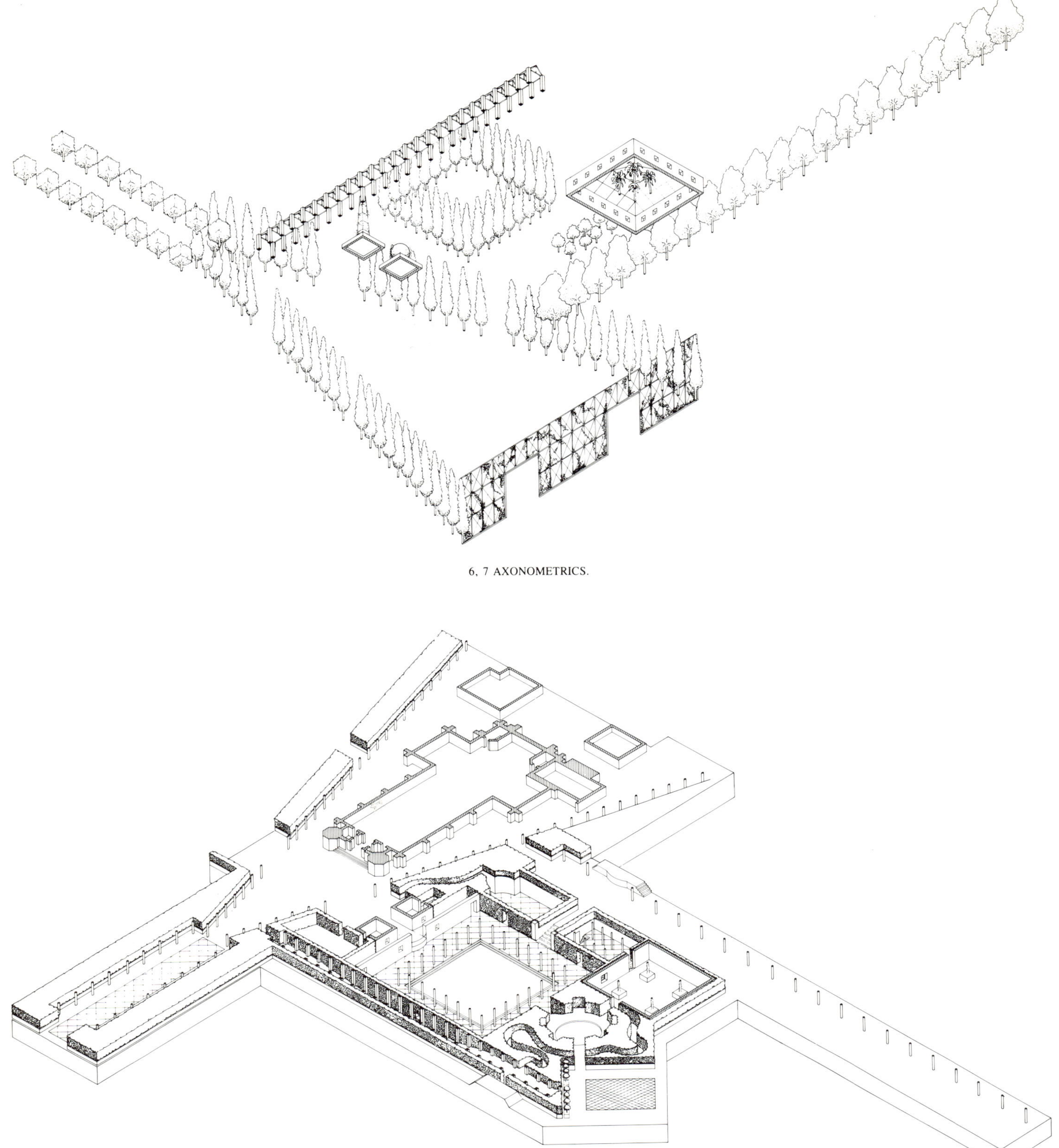

6, 7 AXONOMETRICS.

while our more ephemeral parks and gardens have demonstrated a remarkable permanence. (See for example the durability of Olmstead's Central Park in New York versus the architectural transformations around its edge). In Toronto, Trinity Gardens offers a timely opportunity to make a memorial to our discarded past.

There are precedents. In K F Schinkel's Schloss Glienicke and Park in Berlin, building fragments from distant antiquity were incorporated into the facades of nineteenth-century buildings. Much closer to home, pieces of early twentieth-century Toronto buildings stand in a park setting in Scarborough's Guild Inn.

The discovery of four giant Ionic capitals on the site provided our initial inspiration. We believe these fragments originate from Charles Cobb's magnificient Registry of Deeds and Land Titles building demolished in 1964 to make way for the New City Hall. We propose to augment these pieces with other fragments from notable and recently demolished buildings close to the site. The Guild Inn in Scarborough has provisionally agreed to make the following available to the City: entablatures and capitals from Carriere and Hastings' Bank of Toronto building situated at King and Bay and demolished in 1966; capitals from Clinton and Russell's Imperial Oil building on King Street demolished in 1969; and arched panels from the single-storey wing of Eaton's College Street designed by Ross and MacDonald and demolished in 1976. A selection of these fragments would be positioned within the Gardens firstly as a memory of Toronto's architectural past and secondly to confirm the classical composition of the Garden and its narrative.

ARCHITECTS Marc Baraness, Margot Griffin, Bob Hannah (Hannah-Olin Landscape Architects), Edward Jones, J Michael Kirkland, Chris Radigan, Mark Sterling, Steve Teeple

THOMAS NUGENT
Interior of Hotel Waiting Area
1984 COMMENDATION

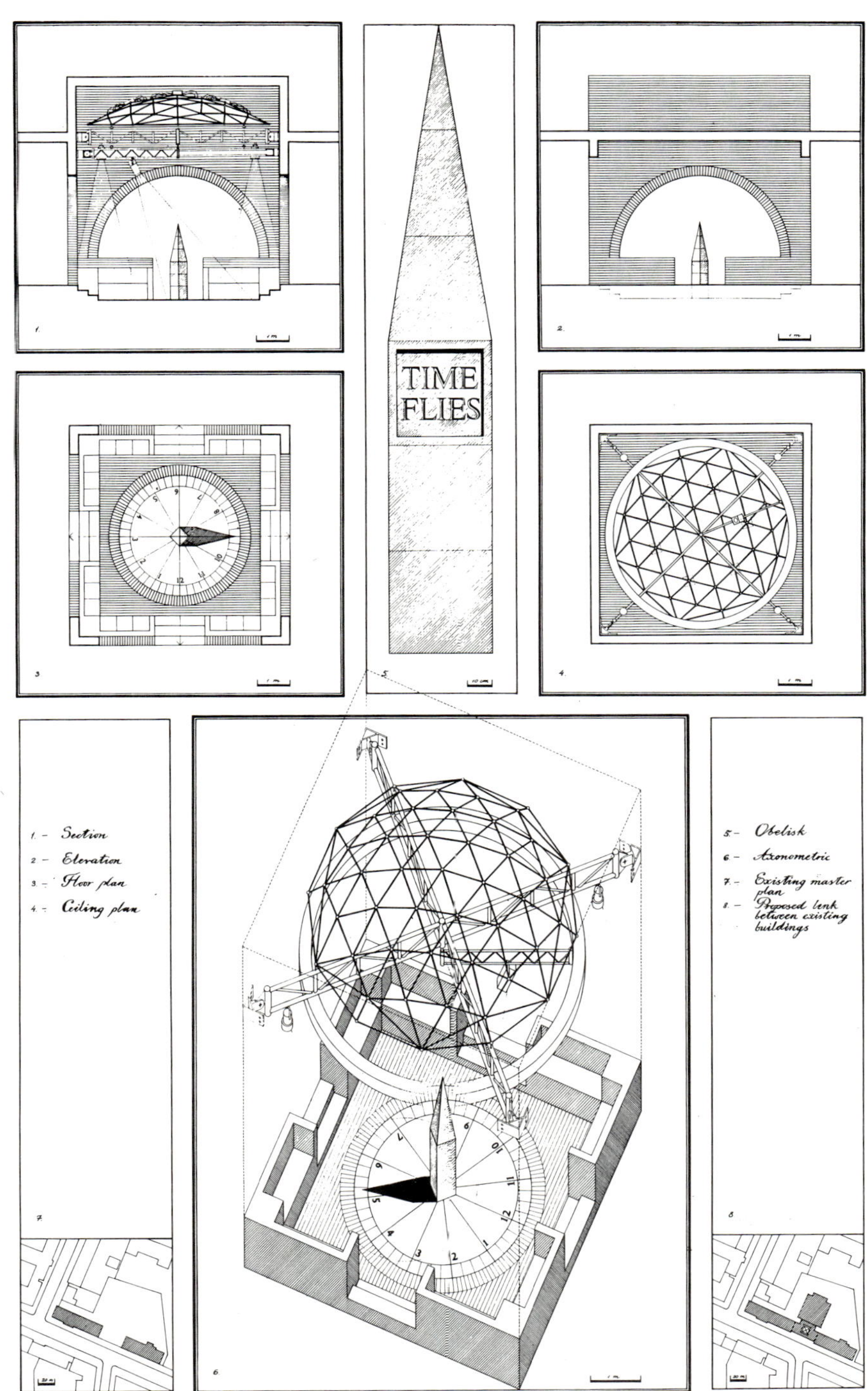

Two existing buildings are to be converted into a hotel, and reception hall, a restaurant and a bar are planned to be added to the existing buildings. The proposed reception hall is placed in the gap between the two building, forming an entrance to the hotel and also serving as a keystone connecting different functional parts of the hotel.

The functional as well as the symbolic importance of the hall is emphasised by a special installation called 'Electric Sundial' which is located in the waiting area of the hall. A frame carrying a cadenza profile spotlight in the ceiling moves around an axis at a speed of one full circle per 12 hours. The shadow of a marble obelisk in the centre of the area shows the exact time on a floor dial; the obelisk is surrounded by four groups of seats. A spotlight (200 par 46 200w light) is fixed above each group of seats. There is also a space-frame cupola above the main diagonal frame with seven boxes of fibre optics used to imitate stars and clouds. 'Electric Sundial', like a traditional clock, is intended to be a convenient place for friends to meet.

SHEILA O'DONNELL & JOHN TUOMEY
House at Ballyweelin, County Sligo, Ireland, 1983

1984 AWARD

1 GENERAL PROSPECT.

This family house is situated on a hillside facing south towards the sea, about three miles outside Sligo town. The intention was to build a house into the hill and to give it a simple, strong form so that it resembled traditional barns or farm buildings in its relationship with the land.

The entrance and living rooms are on the upper level. Within a rectangular plan there is a sequence of three main rooms, (kitchen, hall, living room), each differing from the others in proportion, axis and daylighting. The living room at the end of the sequence has large windows to the east and west. On either side of the timber fireplace, french doors open onto the south-facing covered terrace. The terrace is connected by an external stair to the ground.

On the lower floor are four bedrooms and two bathrooms. Each bedroom has east light and the master bedroom looks south to the sea. On the west side a glazed back door with window seats connects this floor to the external stair leading to the terrace.

The house is made of concrete block cavity walls roughcast-rendered and painted cream; the string course and base are smooth-rendered and painted grey. There are painted hardwood casement windows and stained timber trusses and railings.

ARCHITECTS Sheila O'Donnell & John Tuomey
CLIENT Bryan and Maire Armstrong
CONTRACTOR Sligo Construction Ltd

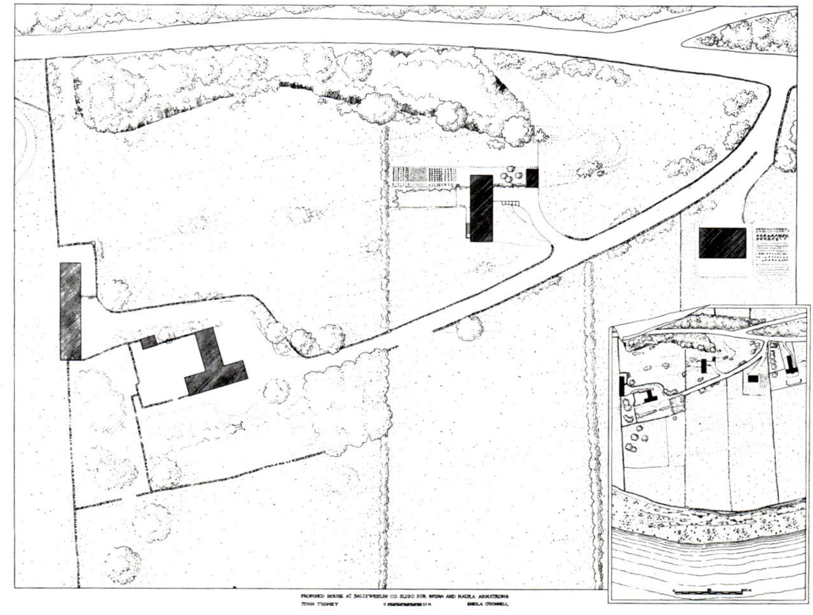

2 SITE PLAN.

3 SOUTH ELEVATION.

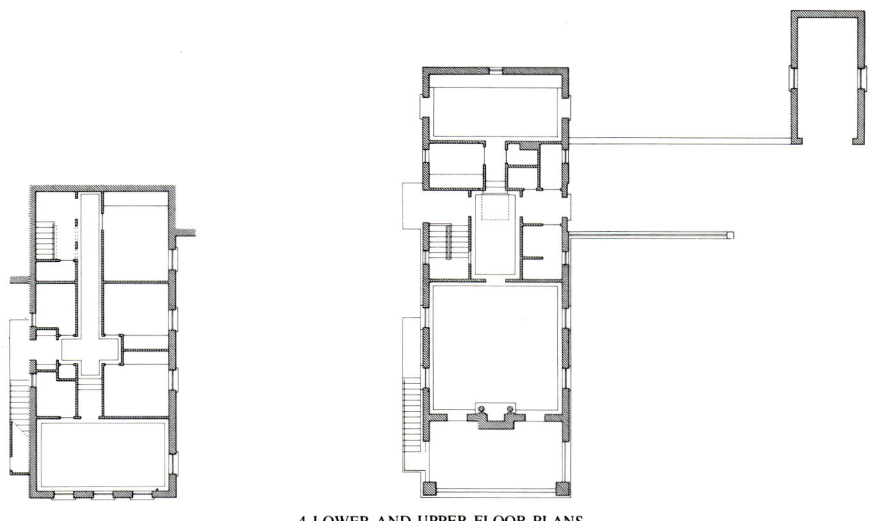

4 LOWER AND UPPER FLOOR PLANS.

5 LIVING ROOM.

ABC ARCHITECTS & BUILDERS

Spring Street Theatre, Spring Street, Hull 1983

1984 AWARD

1 ENTRANCE FRONT, PHASE TWO.

ABC have produced a two-phase Design and Build Scheme; Phase I is as built, Phase II (for £40,000) to be constructed when house-full notices go up, is indicated on the drawings.

The clients were Hull Truck Theatre Co., who had taken over an existing theatre, formerly the Humberside Theatre. The time limit was three months from the start of design to completion of the contract. The budget was a mere £8,000 and our work was limited to interior design and a new facade. The interior identifies the differing functions of the theatre (foyer, box office, bar and cabaret) with surface finishes and elements fulfilling, reinforcing and occasionally surprising the visiting public's expectations. Thus the foyer contains a tiled floor, free-standing columns, a video monitor which shows extracts of current productions and an illuminated arch to the box office. The box office juxtaposes the elements of front and back stage, appearing to refer to the Art Deco ticket office but, upon exit, exposing the back stage of the scenery flats behind.

The existing bar is re-clad in stainless steel and laminate, the seating consisting of re-used bus seats in booths with tables which refer to the typical 60s cafe and the buffet car of British Rail train (pre-Inter City 125). Posed against the bar is a plaster figure of a well-dressed theatre-goer casually taking a drink. The end wall of the bar is taken up with an adapted set showing an impression of a lower middle-class terrace house, through which the public must pass to go to the toilet.

The cabaret room beyond is dark and poorly lit. It is dominated by the small stage and 'Radio Wall' which is a relief backdrop. Opposite is the food servery which recalls the same cafe as the bar tables but with elements of Art Deco and Star Trek overlaid.

Externally, within the limited budget we tried to recall images of Sunset Boulevard within the 'low structure' backdrop of urban factories and warehouses.

The result, we hope, shows the significance of Design and Build and that Art can be cheap.

ARCHITECTS AND BUILDERS The Architects & Builders Co-operative (Hull) Ltd: Andy Earl, Nick Domminney, Chris Jones, Phil Wren
CLIENT Hull Truck Theatre Company
CARPENTER/ARTIST Dave Whyatt
SCULPTRESS Pauline Jones
MODELS Chris Shaw, Ika Kaminka
NEON SIGN John Spencer Ltd
PHOTOGRAPHY Patrick Shanahan

2, 3 FOYER AND BAR. (PHS PATRICK SHANAHAN)

EVA JIRICNA

Kenzo Shop, Sloane Street; Belsize Park Flat, 1983

1984 AWARD

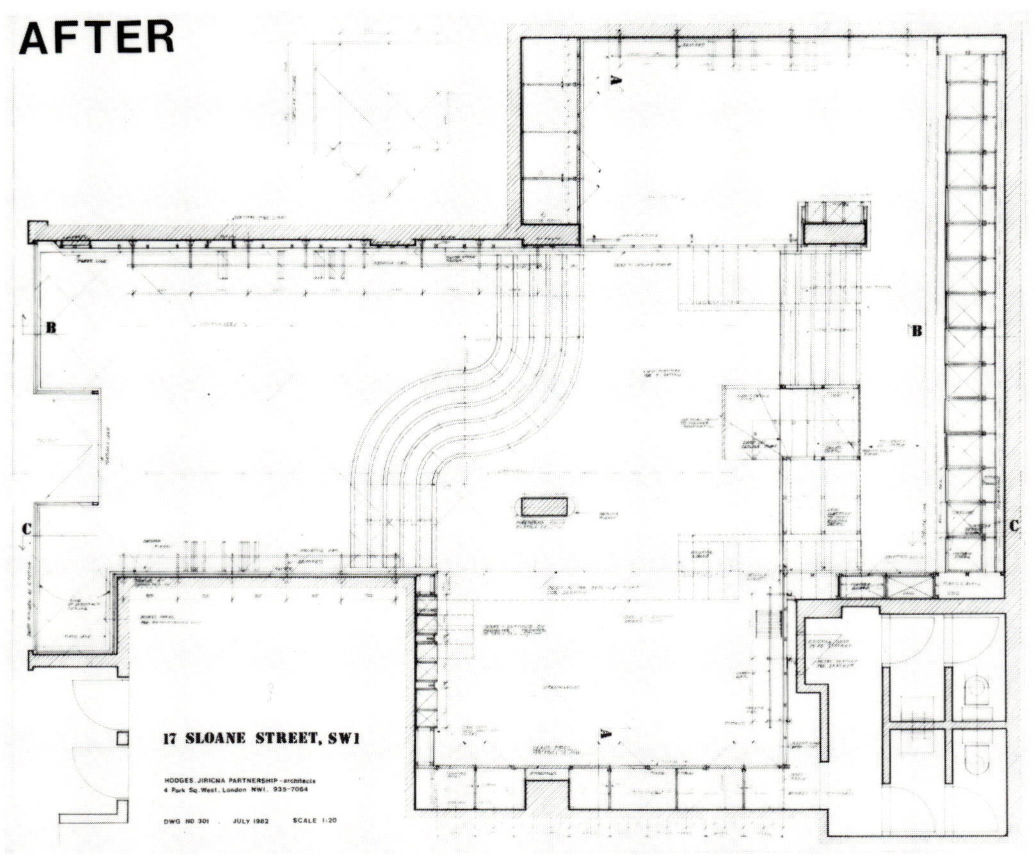

To introduce three levels in order to overcome a problem of great height difference between the entrance level and the upper gallery; to create an atmosphere reminding the customers of the Japanese origin of the designer (Kenzo's requirement); to build a minimum amount of visible obstructions (hanging rails supports, table legs, shelving brackets etc) in order to let the garments and people play the major roles; to create a space similar to a theatre stage design (black ceiling, wooden floor, mirrors, wide stairs etc) for the customers and shop assistants to perform (the dramatic flavour of Kenzo design encourages such thoughts).

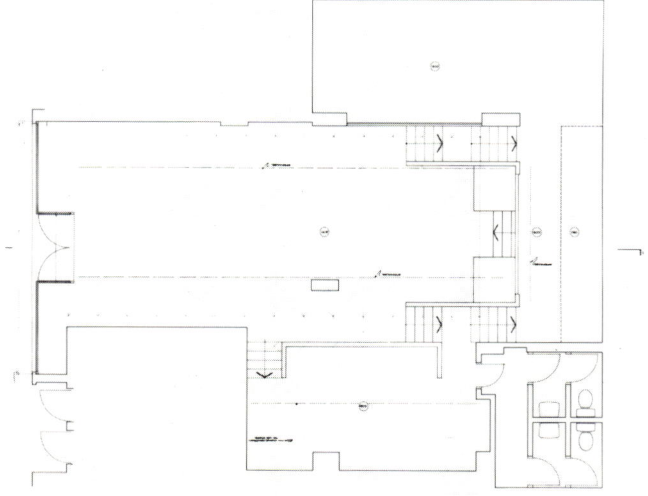

1, 2 PLANS BEFORE AND AFTER RE-DESIGN.

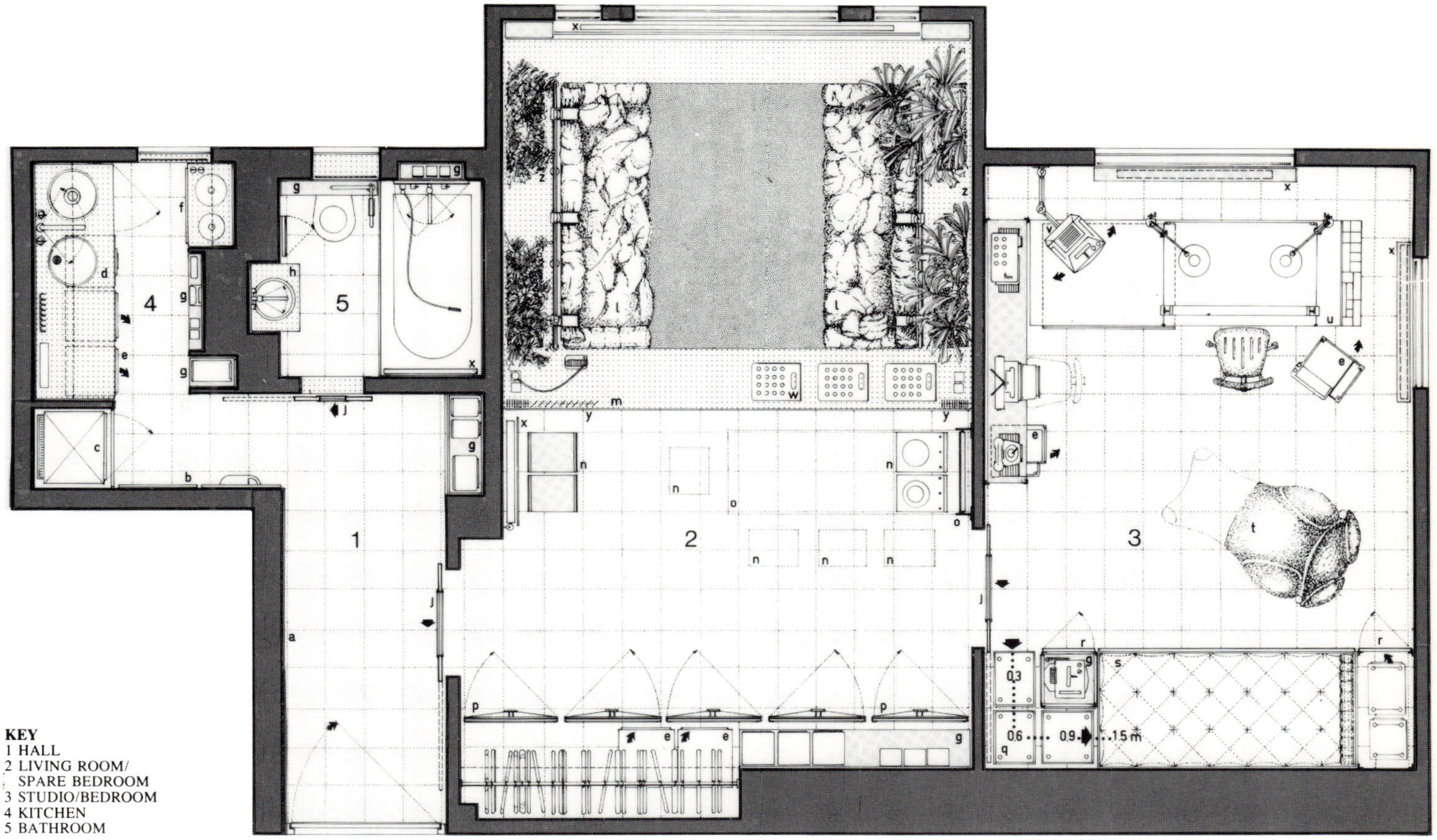

KEY
1 HALL
2 LIVING ROOM/
SPARE BEDROOM
3 STUDIO/BEDROOM
4 KITCHEN
5 BATHROOM

1 PLAN.

Conversion of one bedroom flat, bought in a very bad condition, into living space and studio.

Design Tricks:

A Combined use studio/bedroom (raised bed above plan chests)

B Illusion of a larger space achieved by introduction of mirrors (doors to storage, walls in the hall and bathroom).

C Folding dining table

D Convertible seating/sleeping area

E Convertible seats/occasional tables

F Roller shutters instead of doors wherever possible

G Perforated metal panels partially see-through

H Cable trays used for shelving in order to eliminate intermediate supports

I Walls and ceilings covered with foam-backed PVC or studded rubber to avoid re-plastering and frequent redecorating.

a MIRROR
b PERFORATED PANELS FOR HANGING COATS ETC
c FRIDGE/FREEZER/STORAGE
d WORKTOP WITH SINK AND DRAINER, SHELVES ABOVE
e DRAWER UNITS ON CASTORS
f OVEN, COOKING HOB, SHELVES ABOVE
g SHELVES
h TOP WITH BUILT-IN HAND WASHBASIN, SHELVES ABOVE
j SLIDING DOORS
l SOFA/BED
m LOW BENCH TO PROVIDE ENCLOSURE, BACK SUPPORT, SPACE FOR BUILT-IN PLANTERS
n SEATS/OCCASIONAL TABLE
o FOLDING TABLE .
p PIVOTED DOORS WITH MIRRORS
q STACKING BOXES/STEPS
r CUPBOARDS
s BED, PLAN CHESTS BELOW
t WINK CHAIR
u DRAWING BOARD
v TELEVISION SET ON REVOLVING BRACKET
w INFLATABLE CUSHION
x CENTRAL HEATING RADIATOR
y VERTICAL LOUVRES
z PLANTS AND BUILT-IN PLANTERS

2 VARIATIONS ON LIVING ROOM/SPARE BEDROOM.

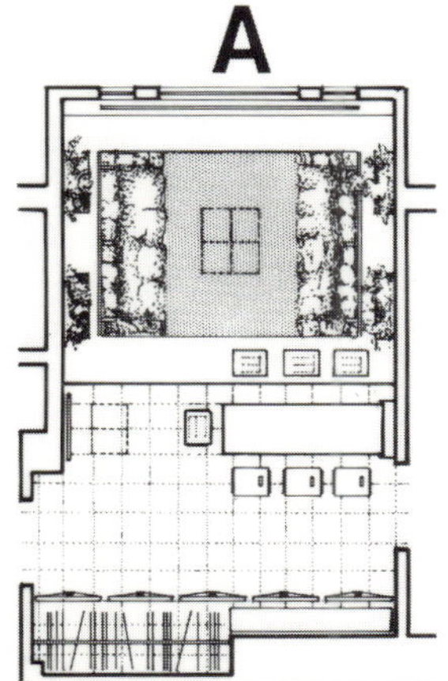

A TWO SINGLE-BED/SOFA ARRANGEMENTS WITH FOUR SEATS/OCCASIONAL TABLES IN THE MIDDLE OR DINING TABLE WITH SEATING FOR SEVEN OR EIGHT

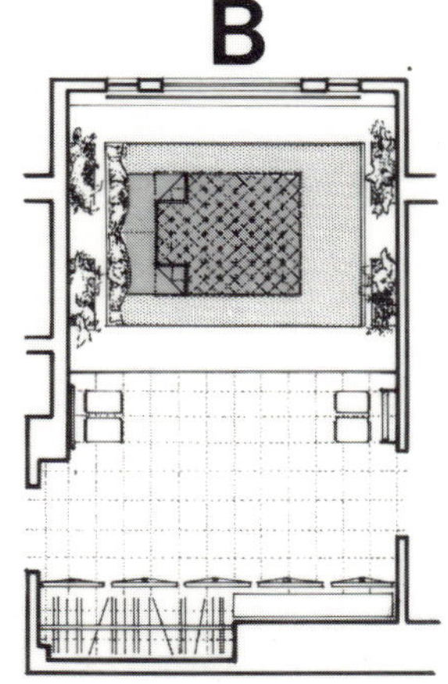

B DOUBLE BED

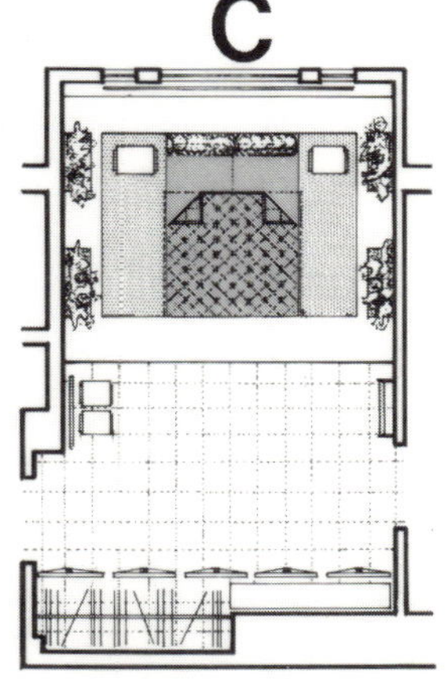

C DOUBLE BED AND TWO BEDSIDE TABLES/ SEATS

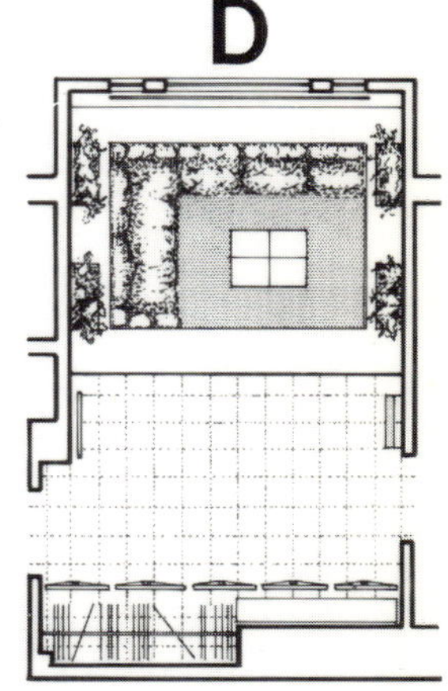

D CORNER SEATING AND OCCASIONAL TABLE/SEATS

3-5 KENZO SHOP INTERIOR VIEWS. (PHS RICHARD BRYANT)

3-5 BELSIZE PARK FLAT, LIVING ROOM, STUDIO AND KITCHEN. (PHS RICHARD BRYANT)

EDWARD CULLINAN ARCHITECTS
New Court, Westoning, Bedfordshire
1983 COMMENDATION

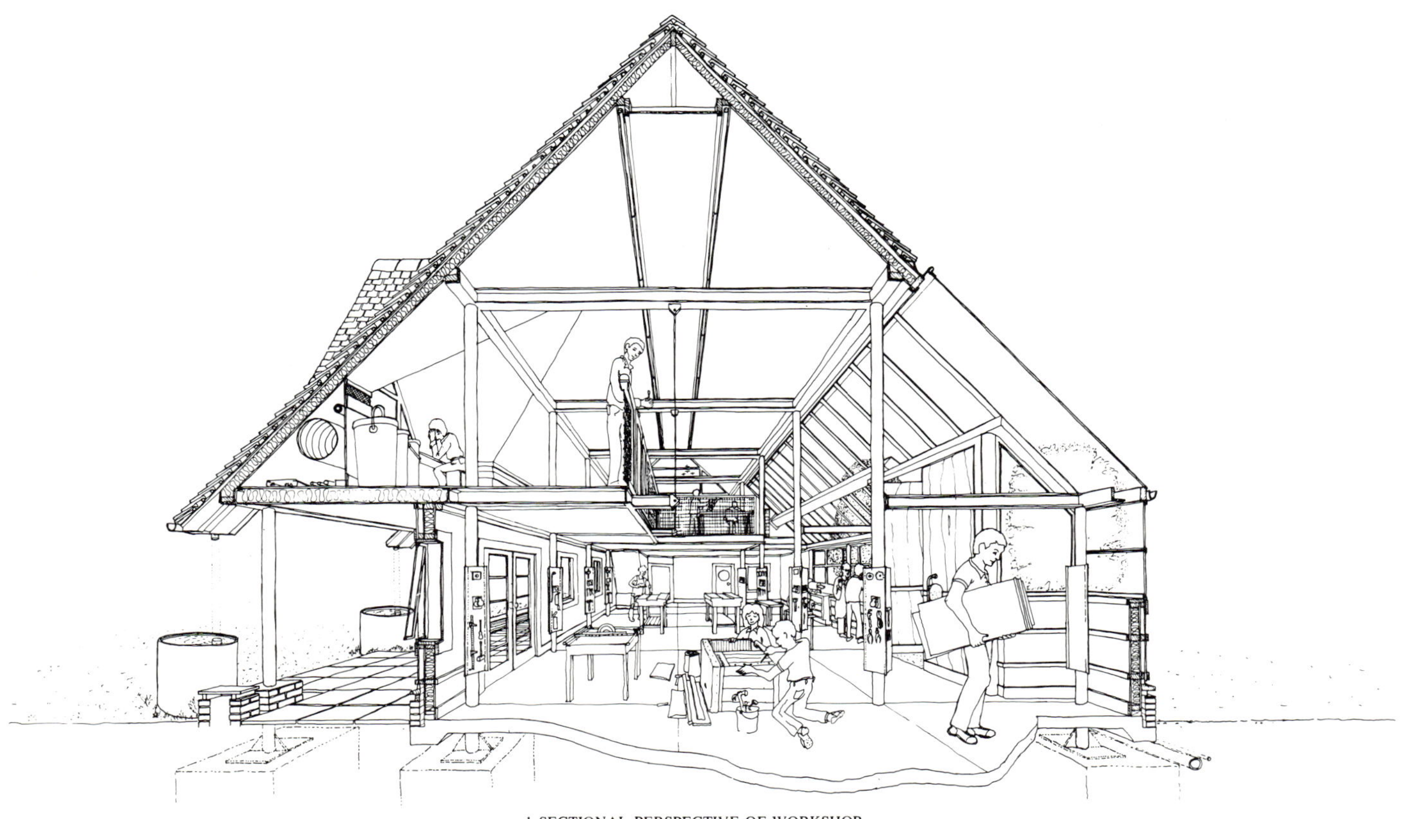

1 SECTIONAL PERSPECTIVE OF WORKSHOP.

A new courtyard

The cloistered courtyard has long been an architectural form that provides both a protected route between disparate spaces and a calm place for contemplation. To extend the community for the mentally handicapped at Westoning around a cloistered courtyard is both to develop the original pattern (the existing manor fronts onto an entrance court behind which lies a large walled garden and a farm court) and to make a place where the residents can walk slowly, sit in peace and play outdoors in all weathers. Fund-raising required there to be separate buildings, one to be built each year.

The buildings' section adopts the 45° pitch of the neighbouring roofs with low eaves or (within which two floors can be accommodated), and into which is cut the deep cloister. Workshops, classrooms and an assembly hall will use the section in a simple linear way, turning it only at ends and entry points. The two houses will cross the section in a more complex way to make corners for the courtyard. We aim to occupy space in a manner similar to the buildings that are already there, but without mimicry or pastiche: jazzily, brightly, lightly, usefully – to stimulate.

Workshop Built

The structure adopted for the workshop is a steel frame, onto which are laid rafters and into which is fitted the first floor. The frame allows the first floor to form a gallery around a central double-height area, providing the necessary connection between the quieter weavers, basket-workers and potters upstairs, and the noisier and heavier metal and wood-workers below. At each end, the lower part of the roof returns onto itself to form two small hips between which sits a large gable window, completing and at the same time revealing the section. The roof thus shelters a large well-lit space which is broken down by the scale of the structure and the frequent views out. The walls are light sandwich panels whose cores were prefabricated by the residents; they are faced both internally and externally by sheet material whose edges and fixings are covered by green cover battens stained ply externally and white melamine inside. The general whiteness inside is used as a bright but neutral backdrop for blue steel, green cover battens and red handrails.

Residence (to be built shortly)

The first corner of the courtyard is turned by a house for ten residents on the ground floor and four staff above. The main cloister entrance on the diagonal leads into the kitchen parlour and games room. Both open into the spacious fireplace hall which forms the heart of the building. Two groups of five bedrooms give off this core: each bedroom has a door that leads onto a small terrace outside and spectacular views over rolling countryside. The staff enter on the opposite corner, the half-landing of their stair making the mantelshelf for the fireplace. Their hallway connects to the ground floor bedrooms but upstairs they are completely private. Upstairs four large bedrooms, a sitting room and dining/kitchen open onto balconies cut into the valleys of the cruciform roof.

As with the workshop, the residents will contribute to the construction of the building with the advantage of the fully equipped workshop alongside.

ARCHITECTS Edward Cullinan Architects
DESIGN TEAM Workshop—Edward Cullinan, Michael Chassay, Robin Nicholson; Residence—Edward Cullinan, Michael Chassay, Robin Nicholson, Gregory Penoyre
CLIENT The MacIntyre Schools Ltd
STRUCTURAL ENGINEERS S Jampel & Partners
SERVICES ENGINEERS Robert Scott Consulting Engineers
QUANTITY SURVEYORS M K Boyden & Co
MAIN CONTRACTOR T&B (St Albans) Ltd

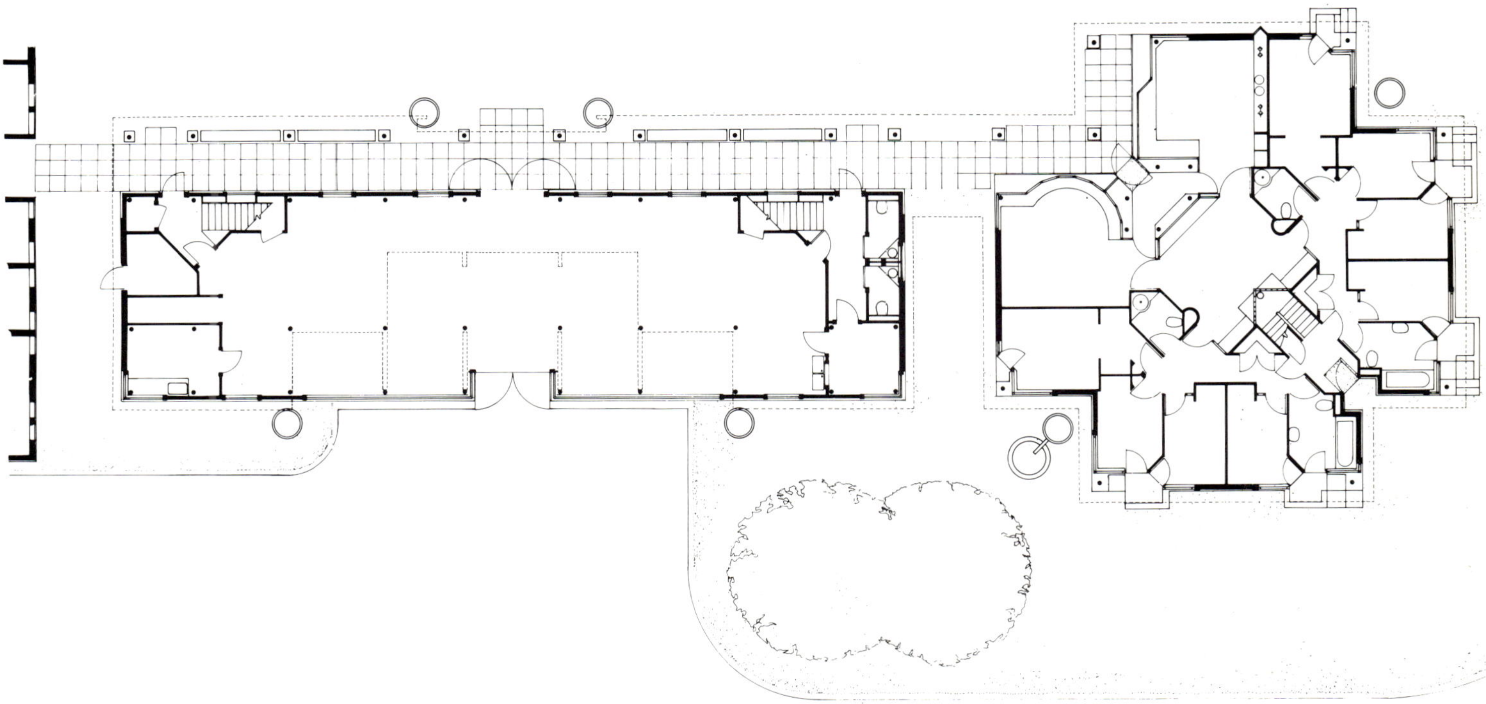

2 GROUND FLOOR PLAN OF WORKSHOP (BUILT) AND RESIDENCE (UNBUILT).

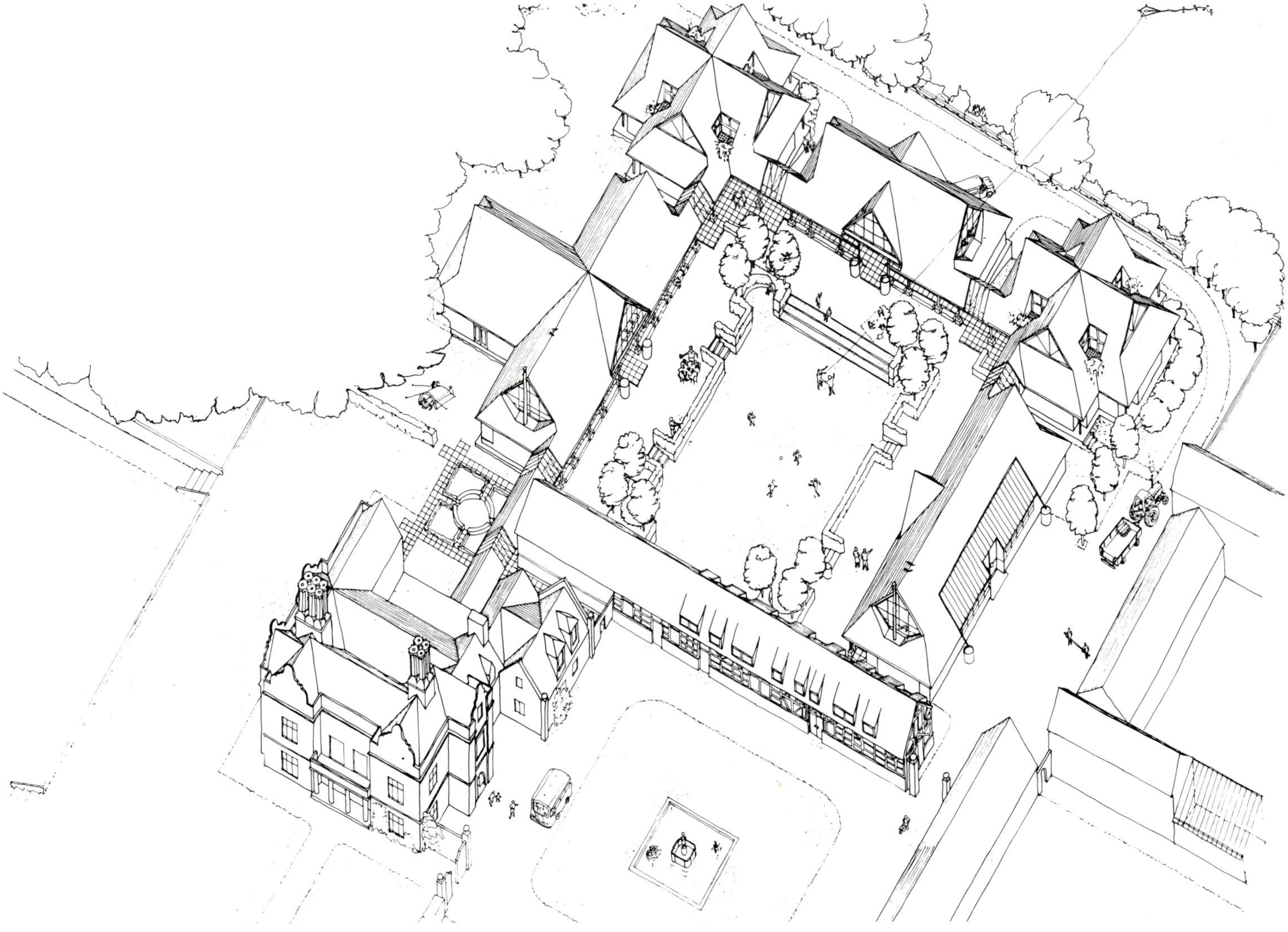

3 AXONOMETRIC OF NEW COURT.

4 VIEW OF WORKSHOP ENTRANCE FRONT WITH RESIDENCE UNDER CONSTRUCTION.

5 COURTYARD ELEVATION.

HAMPSHIRE
COUNTY ARCHITECTS DEPARTMENT
Tadley Burnham Copse Infant School

1984 COMMENDATION

1 DECORATED MULTI-PITCHED ROOFS UNDER CONSTRUCTION. (PH H C C)

2 PERSPECTIVE OF HALL AND CLASSROOM BLOCKS.

3 AERIAL VIEW OF MODEL.

The site is part of a badly run-down area, and an important objective of this design for the Hampshire County Education Department is to provide a strong visual focal point in its redevelopment.

The brief called for a 7-class 245-pupil replacement school with the facility to increase in size to a full 9-class two-form entry school of 315 pupils. The building is a development of an earlier primary school design and consists of a classroom block and a hall block connected by a small glazed link.

To demonstrate that every class forms an integral part of the whole school (a firmly-held philosophical tenet amongst local education advisers), all the classrooms are given equal importance by placing them round a central shared area, thus preventing any sense of visual isolation. This arrangement gives each classroom a long length of external wall and allows for a separate well-lit class base without unduly obstructing the light to the rest of the room.

Two blank segments are included under the roof which will be converted to classrooms when the school is enlarged, but for the present, this area can be used for covered play. Each classroom opens directly onto its own semi-enclosed outside area where teaching can take place on fine days.

The administration and service rooms are grouped around the hall and this accommodation forms the second block, with the main entrances, both for visitors and pupils located at the link.

The tent-like, multi-pitch roof shapes of glass, slate and tiles arranged in decorative patterns are intended to stimulate the imagination of small children, and with the unusual shapes and bright colours within, will produce an environment which may well linger in their memories.

Structure

Load-bearing brick supporting timber purlins and rafters all exposed internally.

Materials

Eternit asbestos slate to lower pitches. Plain tiles by H F Warner to upper slopes.

COUNTY ARCHITECT Colin Stansfield Smith MA Dip Arch (Cantab) ARIBA
DESIGN TEAM Ian Templeton, Ian Lower
QUANTITY SURVEYORS Langdon & Every, Southampton
STRUCTURAL ENGINEERS Brian Veck, Malcolm Gates: H C C
ELECTRICAL ENGINEER Roy Yeoman: H C C
MECHANICAL ENGINEERS David Wright, Derek Yeomans: H C C
LANDSCAPE ARCHITECT Christianne Strubbe: H C C
CLERK OF WORKS Dennis Holloway: H C C
CONTRACTOR W M Annette & Co Ltd, Basingstoke

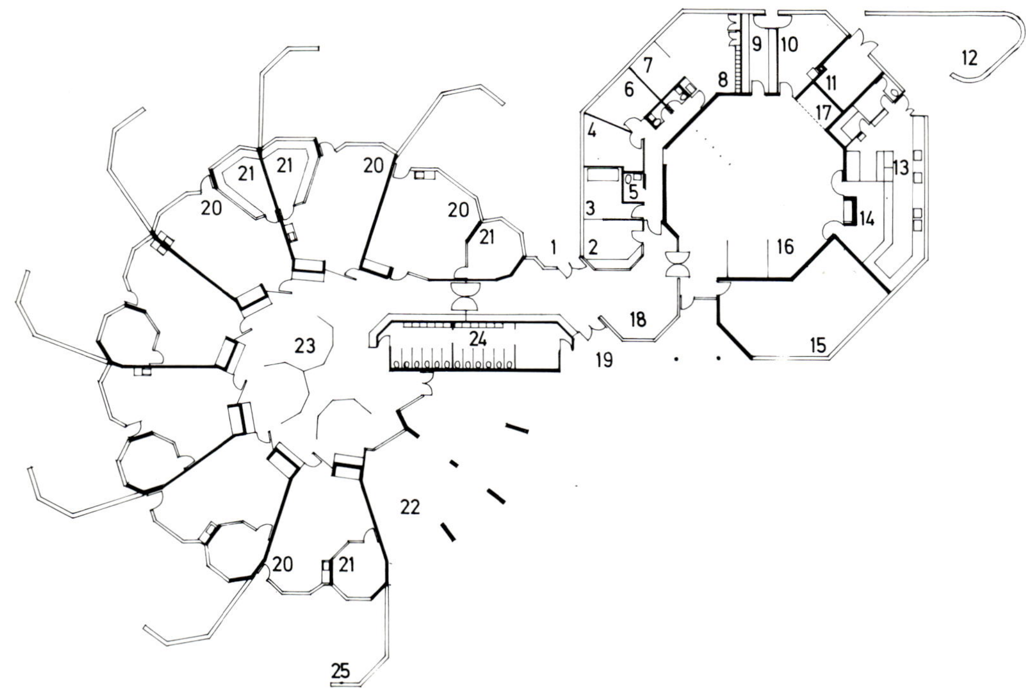

PLAN 1:200

KEY
1 MAIN ENTRANCE
2 OFFICE
3 M I ROOM
4 HEAD
5 DISABLED LAVATORIES
6 DEPARTMENTAL HEAD
7 STAFF WORK ROOM
8 STAFF ROOM
9 STORE
10 CARETAKER
11 PLANT
12 YARD
13 KITCHEN
14 SERVERY
15 MUSIC/DRAMA
16 HALL
17 P E STORE
18 LIBRARY RECESS
19 CHILDREN'S ENTRANCE
20 CLASSROOM
21 CLASS BASE
22 COVERED PLAY—FUTURE CLASSROOMS
23 SHARED AREA
24 LAVATORIES
25 OUTDOOR AREAS

4 PLAN.

FAULKNER-BROWN, HENDY, WATKINSON, STONOR

Chester-le-Street Civic Centre 1982

1983 COMMENDATION

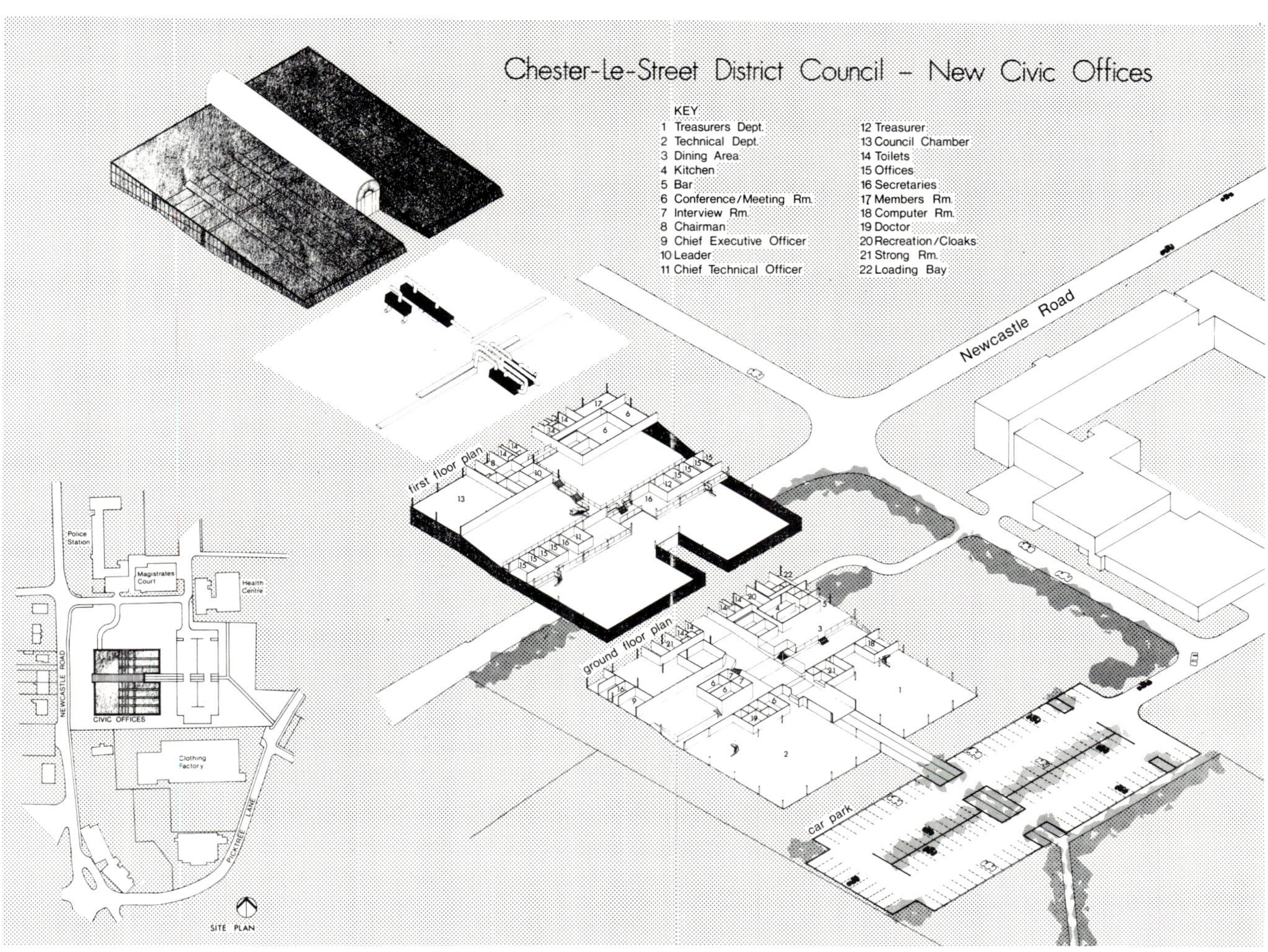

1 AXONOMETRIC.

The nature of the city is being eroded by architects' belief that they have a single responsibility to the client's brief. They thus neglect any responsibility to the public nature of a city and the necessary contribution each and every building has to make. This three-way dialogue between building/user and public is essential to the successful working of any town or city, and nowhere more manifest than in a Civic Hall.

The Victorians expressed this in edifices to civic pride, prosperity and strong authority, as seen in Halifax Town Hall. Today, new civic offices like Hillingdon and South Norfolk reflect a loss of direction and identity in local government with retrospective attempts at vernacular imagery. Chester-le-Street District Council, by contrast, sees itself as working on behalf of the area in an efficient and socially aware manner. We have developed at Chester-le-Street a vocabulary which will express and articulate today's local government requirements as vividly as those developed for Halifax Town Hall in the last century.

Our appointment was to carry out a feasibility study of the current and future requirements of Chester-le-Street District Council. Analysis showed that the small nature of the council necessitated staff to work flexibly between jobs and groupings, and this could best be achieved if all the staff were in one building where flexibility of working could be capitalised upon as opposed to the dispersed nature of Chester-le-Street District Council's present four buildings. To satisfy the complexity of relationships and the need to adapt to present and future usage patterns meant our developing a form which could respond to the hierarchy of changing needs, whilst still retaining an overall coherence.

The site is central to town facilities and has been previously undeveloped. Two natural routes had occurred across the site to the Health Centre, one from the higher western boundary which is essentially formal, and the other from the lower eastern border which is informal, smaller in scale and more random.

Design Solution

Hierarchy of Space—the building space divides itself into:

1. Public Spine—Public
2. Amenity Zone—Semi-Public
3. Private Offices—Private

Central to the organisation was the requirement for a simple method the public could meet the officers. To satisfy this whilst enhancing existing routes and allowing a dialogue between public and local government, a central public glazed arcade runs from west to east off which enquiry counters, meeting rooms, waiting areas and restaurant are located, allowing open government to be seen to be in operation. This arcade can be extended further to the east and offices built alongside if further offices are required. The spine is used as a servant/service people zone where all movement/circulation occurs, heated and cooled air, etc.

Private Offices & Amenity Zones

Three types of office accommodation are required:

a) burolandschaft	55%
b) cellular related to (a)	10%
c) private cellular—council suite service area	35%

This accommodation is layered across the site within a large silver wedge-shaped shell, falling from a two-storey section to the west to a single-storey in the east; the private cellular offices are in a two-storey zone running north/south to the west of the site, separated from the burolandschaft space to the east by an amenity zone for restaurant, meeting rooms with full trees, rooflights, and creating a dynamic conservatory space onto which surrounding offices can look. We have guarded against future offices requirements for additional cellular offices (related to the burolandschaft space) destroying the open aspect of the burolandschaft space by introducing a mezzanine level on and below which 100% extra offices can be located with minimal disturbance.

This building affords a clear structuring of spaces and degrees of flexibility ranging from the addition of two or three offices to the removal of all the internal demountable partitions. The building use can similarly be tuned for varied uses, eg evening use where the restaurant and arcade could be rented out for functions, discos, etc., affording maximum use for the local area becoming a town facility.

The two-storey zone to the west is a portal frame against which long span lattice trusses in pairs at 7.2 metre centres span to. The roof skin, a silver 'Plannja Energy Roof' (first installation in England), spans the 7.2 metre centres between lattice trusses with a triangular duct carrying the ductwork resting on the twin lattices.

The external wall skin is the result of development work with a proprietary gasket glazing curtain walling manufacturer, and allows the internal and external skin to be zipped in or out independently from one bar, giving greater flexibility and consistency between internal and external forms.

A very rapid programme was required. To meet this, a management contractor was appointed in May 1980. Work commenced in May whilst the design was being developed. To achieve rapid and continuous construction, each element has been developed to be distinct from other elements, forming a loose-fit shell constructed from a 'kit of parts' using an appropriate technology.

ARCHITECTS Faulkner-Brown, Hendy, Watkinson, Stonor
DESIGN TEAM
Partner-in-charge—E C Watkinson, S Hendy
Project Architect—N F Taylor
Contract Supervisor—B R Turnbull
Technicians—S S Brennan, D Whitfield, H Plonka, G Pye, S Baker, D Laws, M Wilkinson
Furnishing—R Peacock
STRUCTURAL ENGINEERS Cundall, Johnston & Partners
SERVICES, ELECTRICAL & MECHANICAL ENGINEERS Cundall, Johnston & Partners
QUANTITY SURVEYORS Gleeds, Newcastle
QUANTITY SURVEYORS, SERVICES Gleeds, Nottingham
LANDSCAPE CONSULTANT H J Lowe
ACOUSTIC CONSULTANT Grootenhuis Allaway Associates
MANAGEMENT CONTRACTOR Northern Division, Wimpey Construction (UK) Ltd

2 RESTAURANT (PHS RICHARD BRYANT)

3 FACADE TO NEWCASTLE ROAD.

4 CONSERVATORY.

5 SPIRAL STAIRCASE CONNECTING BUROLANDSCHAFT SPACE TO OFFICES ABOVE.

BARRY GASSON ARCHITECTS
The Burrell Collection, Pollok Park, Glasgow, 1983
1984 AWARD

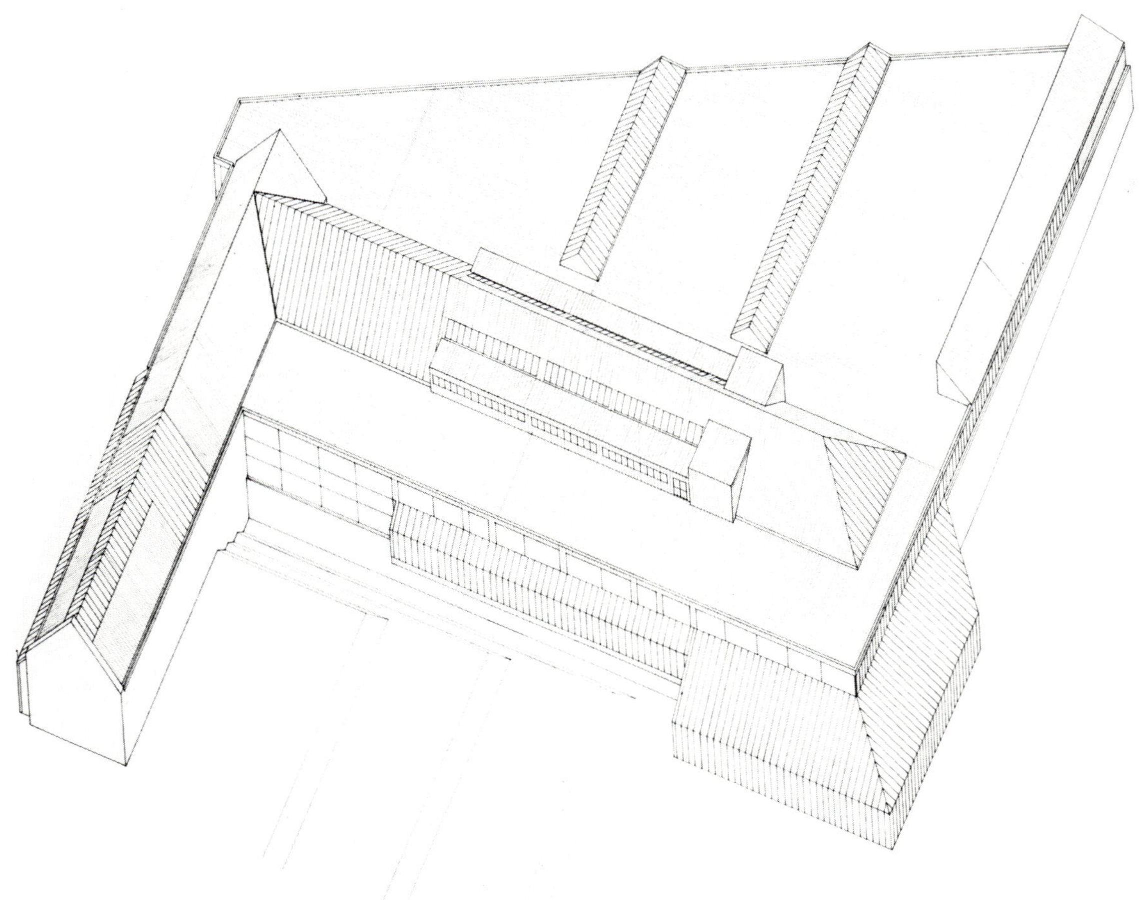

1 AXONOMETRIC.

Sir William Burrell (1861—1958) was a Glaswegian shipowner who presented to his native city the collection of works of art that he had acquired over a very long lifetime. This was to be known as the Burrell Collection. In return the City agreed to provide a new building so that it might be both enjoyed and preserved for time to come.

Burrell collected from Europe, the Middle and Far East, and the collection consists of stone windows and doorways, carved screens, a timber ceiling, furniture, timber and stone sculptures, tapestries and carpets, needlework and lace, stained glass, paintings and drawings, and many objects of stone, timber, metal porcelain and glass. It has breadth of time, of scale and of subject, yet it has integrity. It also consists of pieces from which one can make a building, and the three rooms from his home at Hutton Castle that he requested to be reproduced are a microcosm of the whole.

The site is a field surrounded by trees and woods in Pollok Park, the country estate of Pollok House, some three miles south-west of Glasgow. The building was begun in 1972. It was to be a home for the Collection, yet at that time also had to bridge a cultural gap probably wider than ever before, and this directed many of these initial thoughts. Firstly, the Collection should have a perceptible order: each object should have its place. Secondly, there should be a way of comprehending this extensive and varied collection, and there should be a way of seeing in a visit all or only part of it. A perimeter route was conceived to offer a line of reference from which one could wander, and this route would be connected by two major galleries offering short cuts and aiding orientation. Thus, through these vistas and interconnecting spaces, not only might different parts of the Collection be seen in varying relationships with each other, but the philosophy of the display and the integrity of the whole might be understood.

Thirdly, the external world should penetrate the building, introducing the changing seasons and the changing day. The glass edges and the north-south daylit galleries enable natural light in varying and controlled qualities to pervade the whole building. The building against the trees enables the inside and outside to become one and for objects to be seen and contemplated in a natural context, making them both a delight to behold and suggesting their essence. There is also a relationship between the ordered building and this natural world and the transition is symbolically on the forest edge.

Fourthly, as only part of the Collection can be shown at one time, there is a need to accommodate a changing display. In respect for these objects, rather than to provide spaces that could change, the building has spaces within it with differing qualities of location, light size and finish. In this way it is hoped that certain places would suggest themselves for the location of certain objects, and the semi-open plan would create juxtapositions that were both intentional and surprising. In a sense this would reinforce the idea of the building being a home as well as an exhibition.

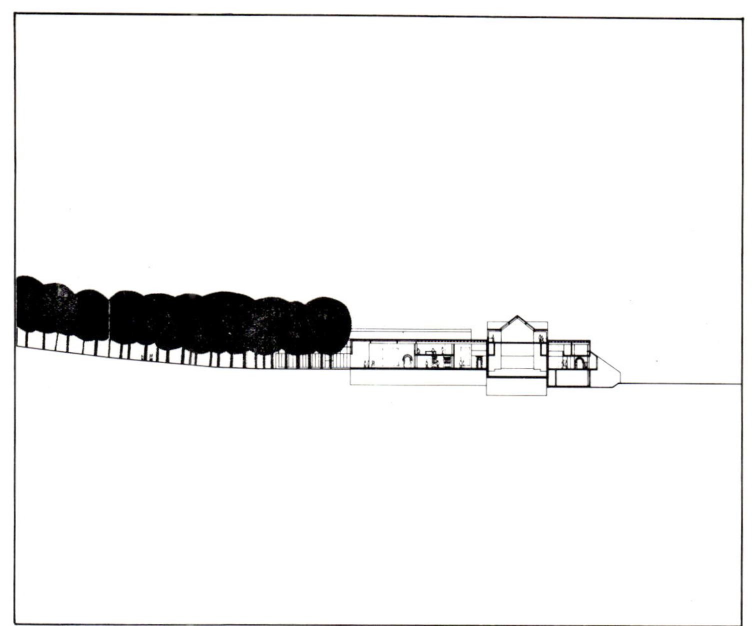

2 SECTION NORTH-SOUTH.

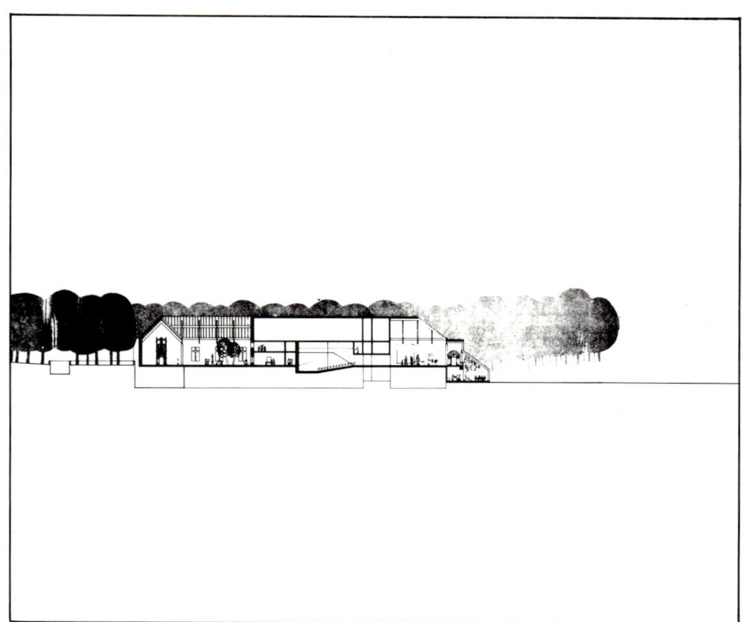

3 SECTION EAST-WEST.

Fifthly, the nature of a work of art in such a building is as intriguing now as in the beginning. How does one display a stone portal, once a doorway and now a piece of sculpture, once outdoors and now indoors? What is a piece of stained glass that once had location and message, and now is history to be preserved forever? How does one display objects of one epoch in a building that denies many of the qualities of that epoch, where the object tends to be explicit while the building tends not to be, and how can the visitor experience these objects when, of necessity, protection from light and touch intervenes? These questions and ambiguities inevitably become part of the building.

To support these thoughts the building is constructed from materials that are basic and have traditional associations. The floors are mainly stone with some areas of timber and carpet, the walls are stone or plaster, and over the whole spans a laminated timber and boarded roof. Into this fabric are woven the complex services that control light and air, and provide protection.

The display of the Collection is primarily on one level, the level of entry and the surrounding woods. In the centre of the building there is a glazed courtyard around which are the three Hutton Rooms and a lecture theatre which is linked to a large gallery for events or frequently changing exhibitions. The perimeter walk extends through the large English sixteenth-century Hornby Portal in the courtyard, past the woods along the north wall where there is a selection of objects from the Collections of Ancient Civilisations, China and Medieval Europe, down through the picture gallery, around the south-east corner overlooking the restaurant, and returning along the stained glass gallery to the south. In the centre there are the halls for tapestries and carpets, and the two daylit galleries containing oriental ceramics and medieval decorative arts. Two mezzanines, one to the north for study or further display, and one to the south for offices and staff, overlook the galleries and provide intimate spaces underneath. Conservation studios are at roof level, and in the basement are workshops, stores and service plant rooms. In total the building is a fully working museum for the display, dissemination, and conservation of the Collection. Yet it has been those aspects of display that have been the most intriguing, working with objects out of time and place, and hoping to make richer the experience of each object and the Collection as a whole.

ARCHITECTS Barry Gasson Architects
CLIENT Museums and Art Galleries, Glasgow District Council
STRUCTURAL ENGINEERS Felix J Samuely & Partners
SERVICES ENGINEERS James R Briggs & Associates
QUANTITY SURVEYORS Davis Belfield & Everest
MAIN CONTRACTOR Taylor Woodrow Construction (Scotland) Ltd

4 SITE PLAN.

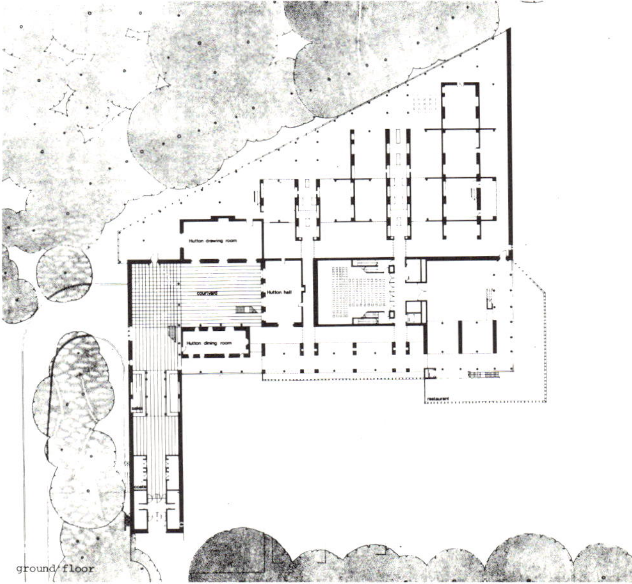

5 GROUND FLOOR PLAN.

MICHAEL HOPKINS ARCHITECTS
Enclosure to Basildon Town Square
1983 COMMENDATION

1, 2 VIEWS OF THE MODEL.

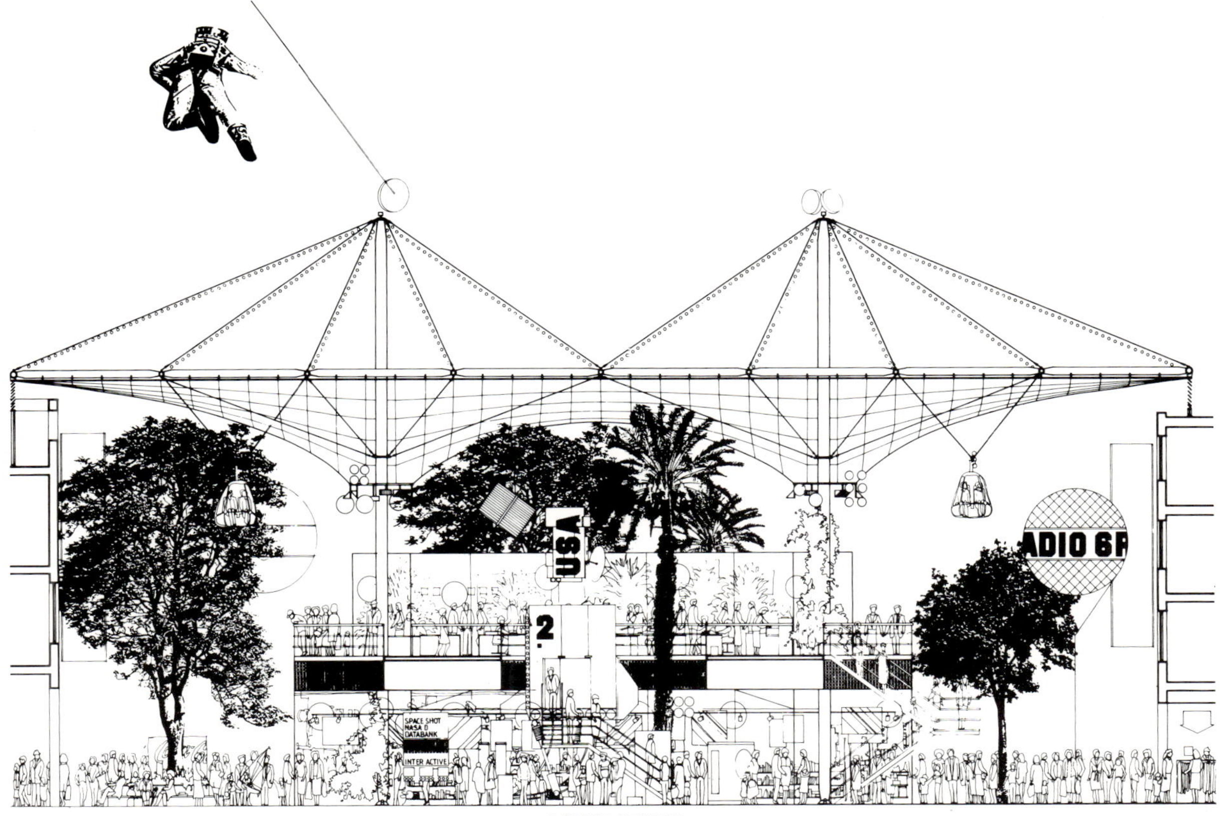

3 CROSS SECTION.

Brief

Our brief was to design an enclosure over Basildon's existing open Town Square. Our major priorities were to:

a Provide weather protection and improve the climatic environment throughout the year.

b Up-grade the level of finishes, furniture and planting.

c Reinforce the town square as the symbolic heart of the town.

d Promote shopping as an enjoyable and entertaining activity.

Roof

The roof is supported from steel columns generally on a 15 x 15 metre grid sited in the middle of the square. A grid of tubular steel booms is suspended from the columns by tension cables and this portalised framework oversails all existing roofs.

A lightweight membrane is tensioned beneath the boom structure in a form that ensures stiffness while held in double curvature. The membrane is divided into 15 metre bays along the length of the square and is fastened along the perimeter of each bay of the structural framework and drawn downwards around each column, fastened to a 'crows nest' platform. The level of the membrane varies between 11.5-15 metre above mall level, forming a naturally vaulted profile rising to high points between structural bays, where there are continuous strips of transparent automatic smoke vents which operate in conjunction with inlet louvres above mall entrances. The membrane consists of a teflon foil-coated glass fibre gridweave which is substantially transparent and has very good characteristics for durability, strength, maintenance, fire, thermal environment and planting considerations. The gap between the roof and the existing buildings will be closed with automatic-opening infill glazing suspended from the roof structure and providing natural ventilation in conjunction with inlet louvres above entrances to the square. End walls will be full-height glazing with doors for the full width of the mall entrances and inlet louvres.

Environment

The town square will be completely weather protected. The environment will be tempered naturally, producing comfortable conditions all year round. It is not intended that the environment will be artificially static, rather a natural climate of contrasting seasons. Naturally lit, the feel and nature of the town square will be light and airy. The malls will be more akin to open streets than the more conventional, artificially lit shopping malls. These proposals constitute an extension of the Victorian principles and language of the arcade, the temperate house and the railway station. Climate structure and fine performance are modified within the context of a contemporary solution utilising appropriate materials.

Focus

Basildon town square has and will continue to have the dual function of town centre and shopping centre. The aim of this project is to bring the town square of the 1960s up-to-date using current technology to create a modern centre for a modern town. The square must therefore become both a thriving shopping centre and the focal point of the surrounding communities. Both shoppers and casual visitors should be drawn to this unique development, incorporating the following attractions, which elevate shopping to entertainment.

Features

Ride: A chair-plane ride will provide a trip through the roof of the centre, passing a story-line of audio visual displays applied to the otherwise dull existing facades. With the primary function of a 'joy ride', it will however serve to transport visitors from one end of the centre to the other.

Garden: The modified climate facilitates the growth of exotic and luxuriant plants, a year-round indoor park with water features and escapist clearings.

Lighting: Lighting will play an important part in both guiding visitors to the centre, and emphasising the sense of place. Searchlights and the neon delineation of structure will identify the centre from the surrounding countryside. Colour coded 'neon lines' keyed into electronic maps, will depict primary routes, leading people from car parks, bus and rail stations through to the town square.

Exhibitions: Temporary exhibitions will be displayed in activity areas. Local firms would utilise this facility with promotion campaigns and sponsored events. Various attractions such as the local and internationally famous marching bands would be encouraged to perform in the town square. Street performers, theatre workshops, local celebrities etc. would also find a forum.

ARCHITECTS Michael Hopkins Architects
DESIGN TEAM Michael Hopkins, John Pringle, Peter Romaniuk, Bill Taylor, David Sparrow
STRUCTURAL ENGINEER (substructure) Chief Engineer: Basildon Development Corporation
STRUCTURAL ENGINEER (superstructure) Michael Dickinson: Buro Happold
SERVICES ENGINEER David Mumby: Buro Happold
QUANTITY SURVEYOR Richard Thomson: E C Harris & Partners
FIRE ENGINEERING Margaret Law: Ove Arup & Partners; Michael Green: Buro Happold

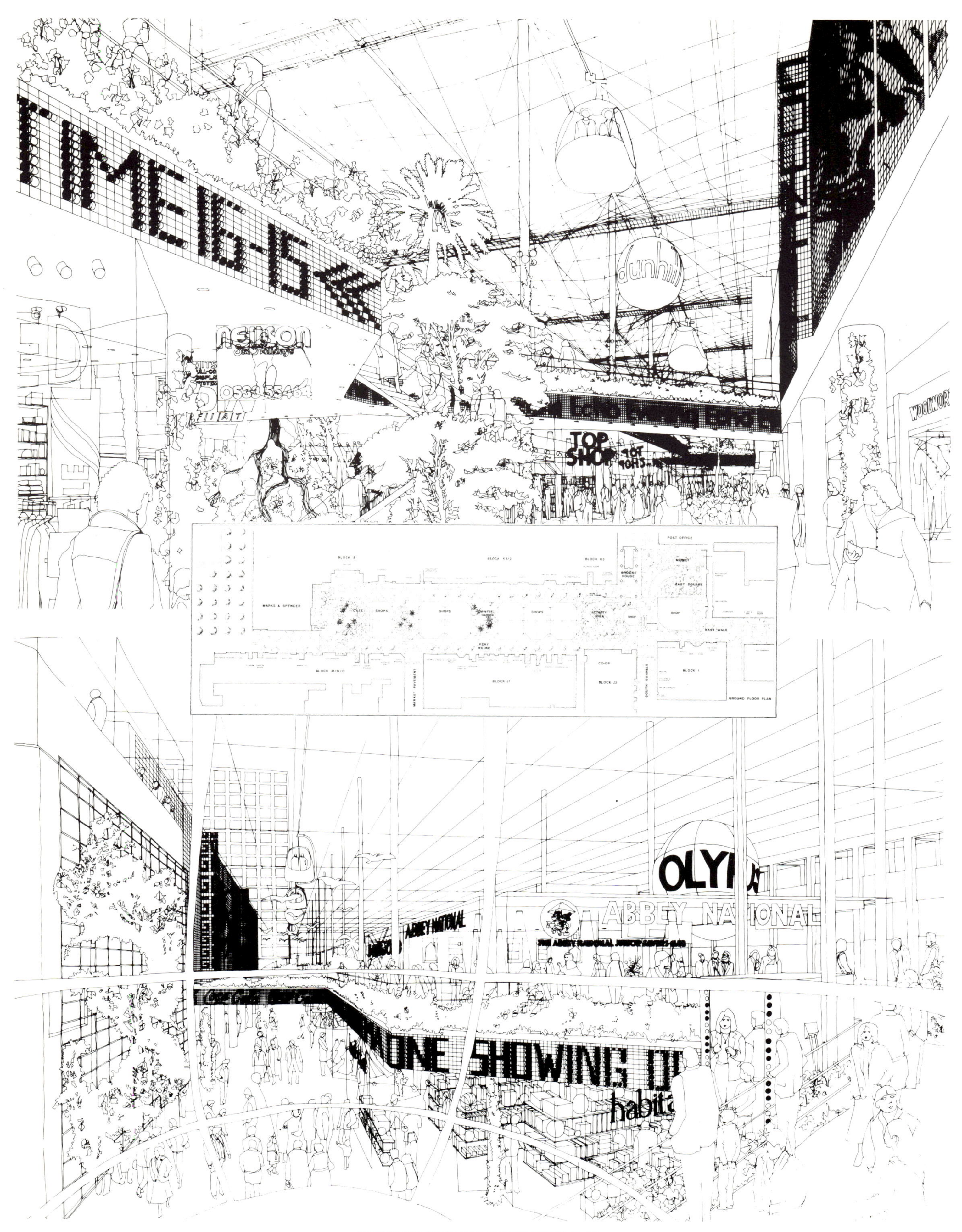

4-6 INTERIOR VIEWS AND GROUND FLOOR PLAN.

IAN RITCHIE ARCHITECTS
Eagle Rock House, Sussex 1982

1983 AWARD

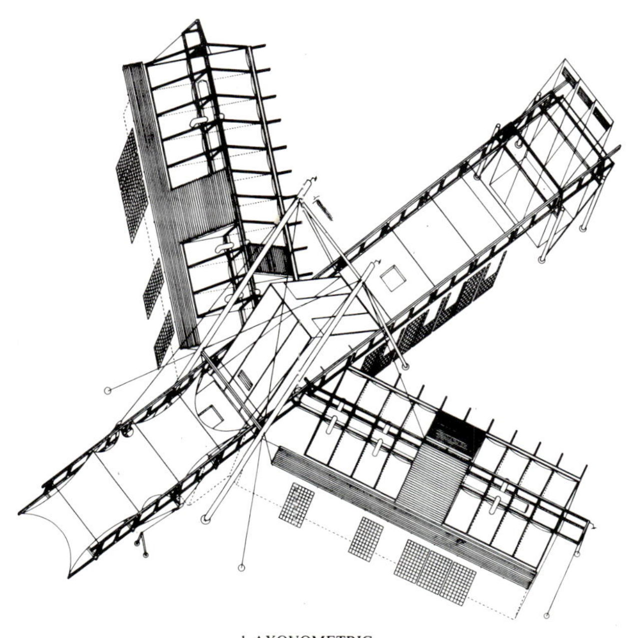

1 AXONOMETRIC.

This house has been an essay in sequential space, its geometry and its modulation by light and shade.

The client's wish for the form of a bird is translated through the articulated structure and the suspension of the wings; the tail as a trapped 'crystal greenhouse' with its protected plants as a counterpoint to the 'natural' landscape of oaks, holly, and sandstone; the movement of the external blinds as a play on the ruffling of the bird's feathers; and the loft space (the bird's head) the focus and energy centre of the house.

The design differs from its original concept in the treatment of the external surfaces. It was originally conceived as a sculpture whose planes, structure and joints were articulated in primary colours (like a Rietveld chair). This idea slowly changed into one of camouflage using a subtle combination of autumn colours and by applying vertical landscape meshes between the garden and the building, attempting to dissolve further the solid planes of the walls and leaving only glass openings through which internal and external spaces are linked by continuous vistas.

ARCHITECTS Ian Ritchie Architects
DESIGN TEAM Hugh Dutton, William Firebrace, Ian Ritchie, Carolyn Steel, Gordon Talbot, Barry Dorson
SITE PROJECT MANAGEMENT Ian Ritchie Architects, Steve Peglau
CLIENT Private client
ENGINEERS Anthony Hunt Associates
QUANTITY SURVEYORS Hanscomb Partnership
LANDSCAPE CONSULTANT Ritchie Chetham Partnership
PHOTOGRAPHY Jocelyne van den Bossche

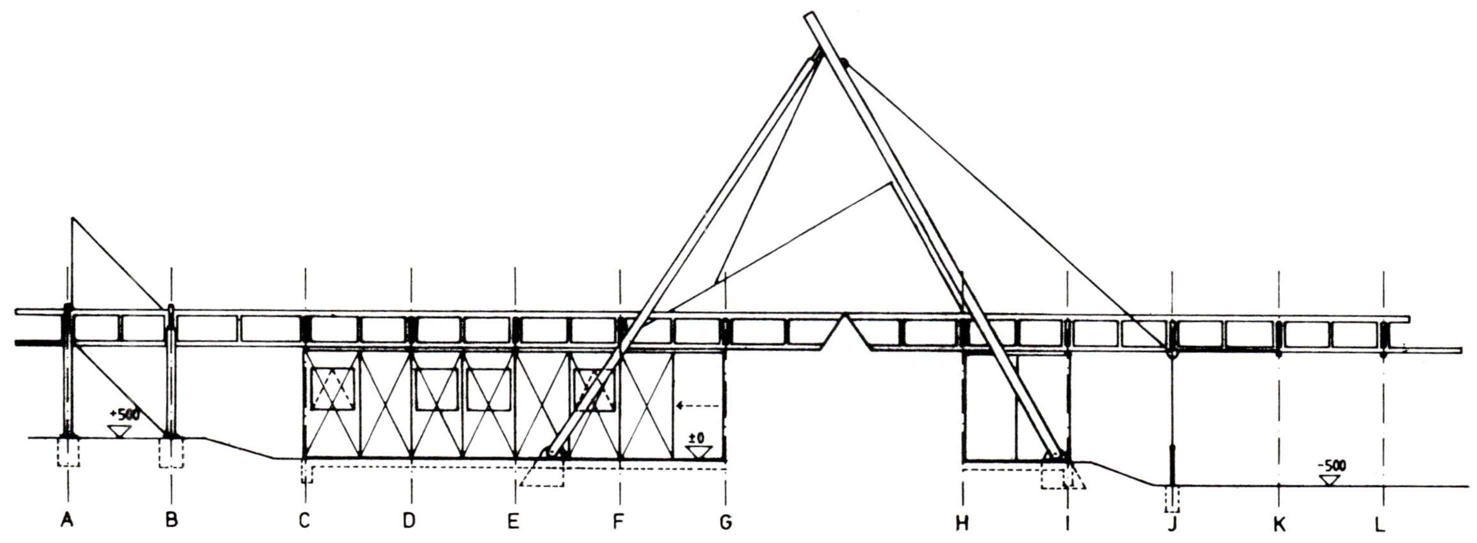

2 NORTH-WEST ELEVATION.

COLIN ST JOHN WILSON & PARTNERS
The City Polytechnic, Hong Kong

1 PERSPECTIVE VIEW OF CENTRAL PLAZA.

This project was one of six finalists in the international two-stage competition for the City Polytechnic of Hong Kong. It is required to serve the day and evening needs of a community of up to 13,000 students and staff, providing teaching, administration, catering, amenity and recreational facilities in planned stages of development.

The site has remarkable physical characteristics, dropping seventeen metres from the principal access road on the east to a central valley and rising again to a public recreational park on the west. Equally dramatic is the towering presence of two mountains: Beacon Hill due north, and Lion Rock due north-east.

A less fortunate aspect of the site is that it lies directly under the flight path of planes landing at Hong Kong airport with the result that there are strict limits on building heights and also a need to protect certain rooms from severe noise interference.

The project preserves as much as possible the organic valley formation within the site for landscape and recreational purposes and focuses its main axial orientation towards Beacon Hill. A secondary entrance from the south-west focuses upon Lion Rock. These are all major factors in the disposition of building elements.

The project responds to certain requirements of the brief by specific architectural means as follows:

1 *A Mall*: a pedestrian promenade flanked by colonnades that provide covered access to the schools which take the form of

2 *Pavilions*: each school is thus physically identified in its superstructure with a main 'front door' on the mall, with its base it is melded into

3 *A Podium*: which houses groups of lecture theatres and non-specialists teaching spaces in such a way that they can be well insulated from external airborne noise, and assigned to a particular school or shared between a group of schools. This option is made possible through the other characteristic of the Podium, namely that it is also

4 *A Concourse*: this affords covered access, at its main level, to the major Lecture Theatres, Schools, student dining and amenity rooms with flanking galleries at an upper level to the minor teaching rooms, staff dining and amenity rooms.

5 *A Central Plaza*: terminates the mall at its southern end in the form of a curved colonnade. This forms the heart of the campus and the focus for academic and community life in which the central library is flanked on one side by the Student Union and on the other by the Central Administration.

6 *Two porticos*: mark the two major entry points to the site, at the south-east and south-west corners. Both announce unambiguously their status as thresholds and both have the capacity to register a memorable image in the mind of the public.

2 MALL PERSPECTIVE.

3 VALLEY ELEVATION.

Organisation of Central Plaza, Lecture and Seminar Rooms

The Departments are disposed along a north-south axis focused upon the horned mountain of Beacon Hill with the departments requiring associated laboratory and studio space ranged along the east (peripheral) flank and so staggered in relation to each other that the eastern range has views between the pavilions of the western range into the 'valley' landscape. The linear distribution makes phased construction both easy to effect while also providing a form that is self-sufficient and intact at all stages of growth.

The steep fall of the site has been used to permit the important south-east entry stair an ascending succession of entry levels to the basement car park, the amenity club rooms, the main concourse, the concourse gallery and finally up to the central plaza. It also provides, very conveniently, a lower stratum of servicing access and car parking separate from the pedestrian networks.

Formal and Symbolic Issues

The academic campus is a major institutional type with a wide range of historic precedents. In this case the decision to establish identifiable department pavilions, linked by covered walkways set against the mountain ranges evoked memories of Jefferson's University of Virginia, focused axially upon the Blue Ridge Mountains. There are also well known precedents in Chinese architecture for the theme of pavilions linked by covered ways. Traditional Chinese values revolving around the theory of the balance of energies that are brought together in the geometric art of Feng Shui are still deeply respected in Hong Kong and failure to meet their requirements can be very damaging. Accordingly, the design carries a number of allusions (not literal but metaphoric) to such traditional motifs as the Five Arch Pai Lou Gateway, the red lattice grille as solar screen (our silkscreen image) and the waterfall and cascade as a feature of the main axis. As a final focus on that axis it was proposed that a facsimile of Brancusi's *Column of the Kiss,* which carries extraordinary similarities to certain ancient Chinese monumental columns, should be placed about the waterfall terrace.

ARCHITECTS Colin St John Wilson & Partners in association with Hsin-Yieh Architects & Associates
CONSULTING ENGINEERS Structure, Building Services, Lighting, Geotechnic, Acoustic: Ove Arup & Partners
LANDSCAPE CONSULTANT Urbis Planning Design Group
QUANTITY SURVEYOR Langdon Every & Seah

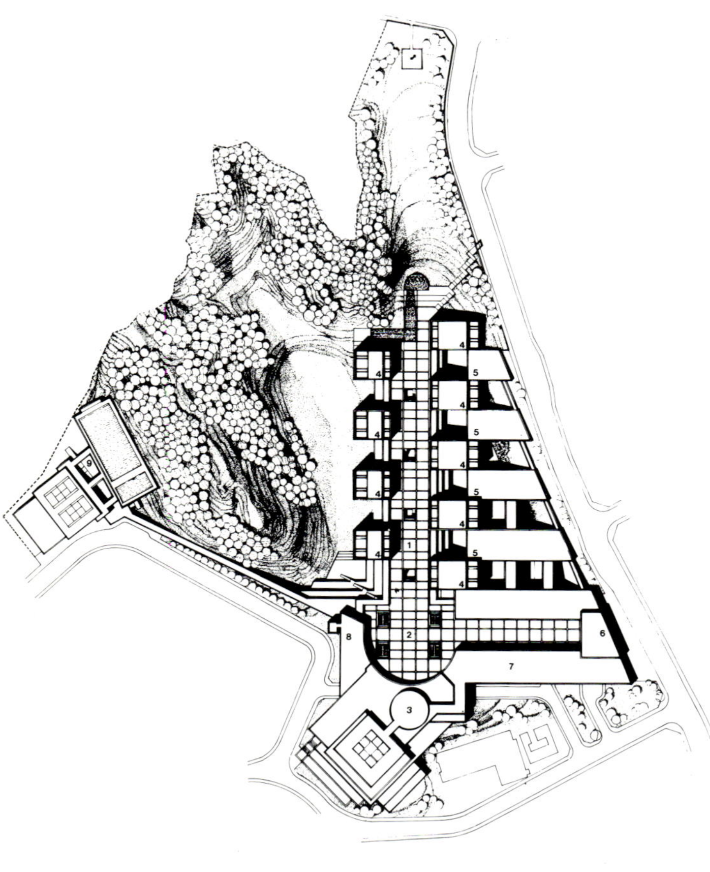

5 PODIUM HOUSING LECTURE THEATRES AND NON-SPECIALIST TEACHING SPACES.

KEY
1 MALL
2 CENTRAL PLAZA
3 LIBRARY
4 SCHOOL PAVILIONS
5 LABORATORIES AND WORKSHOPS
6 MAIN ENTRANCE PORTICO
7 ADMINISTRATION BUILDING
8 STUDENT AMENITIES BUILDING
9 SPORTS CENTRE

4 SITE PLAN.

6 MODEL VIEW FROM VALLEY.

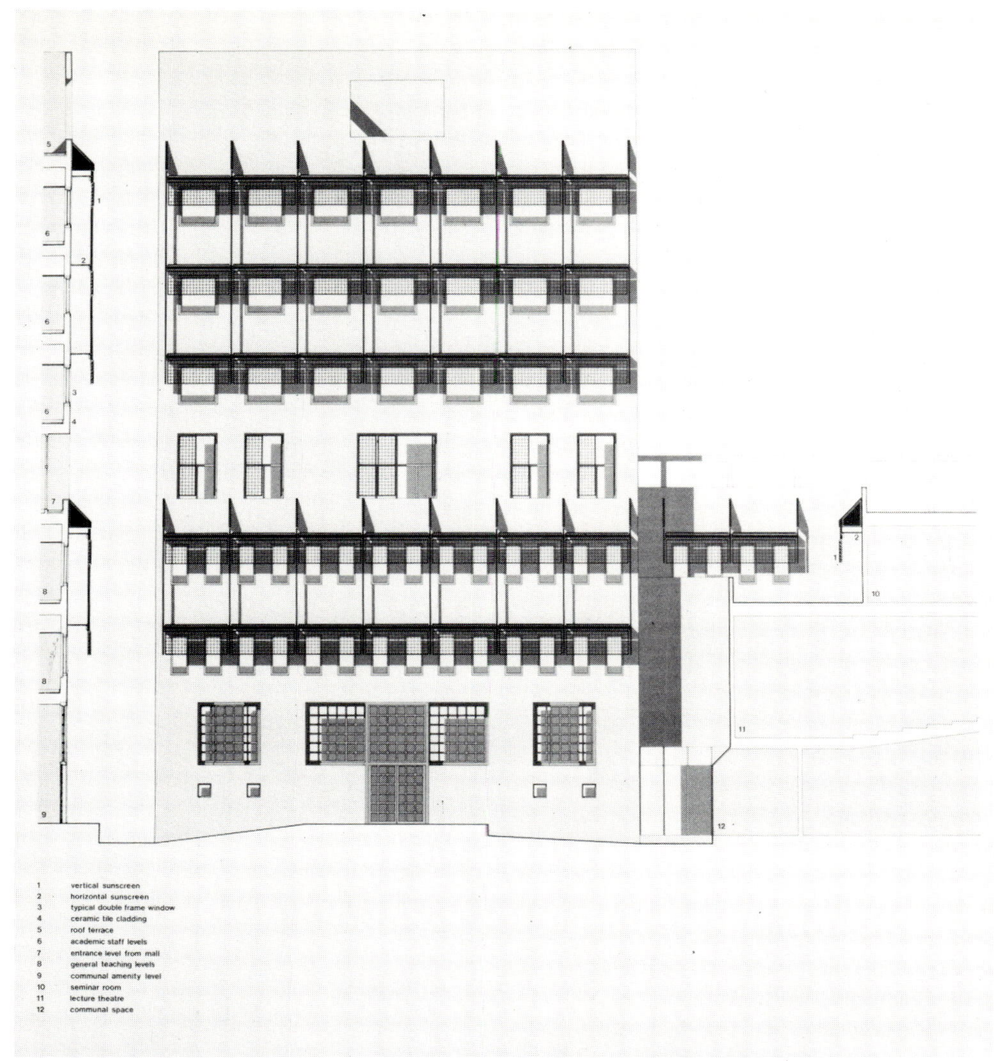

7 SCHOOL PAVILION ELEVATION.

8 CONCOURSE PERSPECTIVE.

JULYAN WICKHAM ARCHITECTS

Restaurant, wine bar and wine shop, Corney & Barrow, London

1984 COMMENDATION

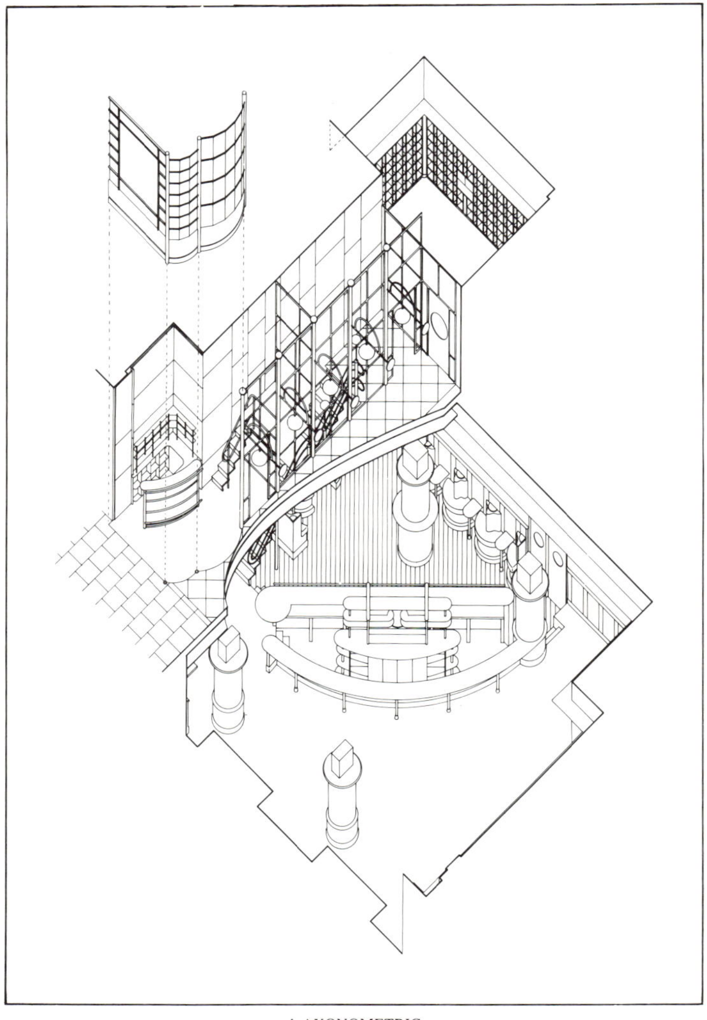

1 AXONOMETRIC.

This recently completed project was for a leading City wine merchant, who, faced with the end-of-lease closure of one of their nineteenth-century wine bars, chose rather than simply relocating their existing type of operation, to go for a more ambitious scheme including a restaurant and their first wine shop.

The site was previously an unlet bare carcass space within a ten-year-old speculative office building built beside and with total disregard for Lutyens' Brittanic House. The tiny facade for the restaurant gave little idea of the space within, being just one of a number of shop units. We have therefore turned the facade into the building along a slate-paved arcade, running past the Champagne Bar on the left, wine showcases on the right, and leading to the Wine Shop and the top of the stairs to the Restaurant and Wine Bar.

The shell had previously been equipped with a staircase and a lift which together incomprehensibly occupied nearly all the space adjacent to the street front. These were removed and a new staircase constructed in a new location. The Champagne Bar occupies the position at the front of the ground floor and steps up over the new stairs to form a 'snug'.

The Wine Shop at the end of the entrance corridor is lined almost entirely with wine bins to allow the display as much as possible of the company's enormous range. The table in the middle of the room was specially designed for the room and has a solid walnut top.

The main staircase is hung from above so as not to clutter the space below. It is of tubular steel construction with aluminium treads and bronze handrails. It lands three steps above the Bar floor level and it is at this carpeted level that the seated Restaurant users share eye-level with those standing in the oak-floored bar.

The ceiling is of purpose-made perforated anodised aluminium panels allowing the conditioned air to filter through without causing draughts.

The walls are panelled at dado level. The plaster above and the round column casings are 'ragged'. The Champagne Bar counter top, the Wine Bar counter top and the curved bar top in the Restaurant area are all made of solid walnut.

With the exception of the chairs all the furniture, fixtures and fittings were specially designed for this project.

ARCHITECTS Julyan M Wickham Architects
DESIGN TEAM Julyan Wickham, Desmond Lavery and Tess Wickham
ASSISTED BY Douglas Streeter, John Somerville-Large, Gillian Scampton, Jamie Campbell and Simon de Wrangel
METALWORKERS T&R Pembroke Engineering (Reading) Ltd
FIRE PROTECTION ENGINEERS RMD Fire Control Limited

2-5 VIEWS OF THE CHAMPAGNE BAR, STAIRCASE AND RESTAURANT BAR. (PHS MARTIN CHARLES)

DE BLACAM & MEAGHER

Projects

1983 COMMENDATION

1 SHELBOURNE HOTEL, GROUND FLOOR BRASSERIE.

Shelbourne Hotel
The proposal for the conversion of the ballroom to an atrium-type brasserie was commissioned by Trust House Forte. The existing ballroom entrance would be converted to foyer and cloakroom space, the ground floor paved with stone and filled with tables, chairs and trees in terracotta urns, whilst the existing roof would be replaced by an opening glass roof with mechanically-controlled spinnaker cloth awnings draped underneath. There would be a servery, a bar, first floor 'private' boxes for dining, and a large pipe organ overlooking the space for noon recitals.

Another proposal for the same hotel was the restoration of its principal dining and meeting rooms overlooking St Stephen's Green, a scheme which called for the entire re-planning, re-servicing, redecorating and refurbishing of the rooms. The major structural changes introduced were secret interconnecting doors and dados. The paintwork varied throughout but consisted entirely of hand-finished work with ragroll, marble and stipple finishes. Carpets and curtains were designed, and window boxes planted with coniferous trees would provide privacy.

Institute of Chartered Accountants in Ireland
This project comprised the members' facilities around a winter-garden, the students' facilities around the library and Institute offices and council rooms around the atrium. All accommodation is organised around the central atrium or hall approached through a conservatory and entrance lobby. The second floor above the atrium is a void to illuminate the entire space by natural light. The library is a galleried room modelled on the Meeting Rooms and Library of the Royal Irish Academy and has clerestory windows between bookcases; additionally, a gallery can be screened off from the rest of the library and used as a classroom. The street facade of the building takes into account the site (the garden of two early eighteenth-century houses), and the proposed architectural treatment would be diminutive and formal.

Effra/European Ferries Cold Stores Site Competition
The design was governed by the surrounding landscape of river, streets, courts and gardens. Offices are conceived as ten courtyards and the apartments as nine detached 'mansions'. The form of the scheme is similar to a palace (like Whitehall) with yards, squares and pavilions. The major portion of the scheme is oriented towards the river, the facade of which is that of a wooded garden screen wall of timber-shuttered and glazed mansion block gables with their balconies of boxed trees. The public entrance to the offices is through a courtyard and formal planting. Finally, there is a retail shopping area conceived as a shopping mall.

Rowlagh Parish Church
The church was commissioned following a premiation received in a 1976 architectural competition held by the Archbishop of Dublin. This proposal was for a new parish church with ancillary facilities; it would have 800 seats and openings in the vaulted roofs over the ambulatory, sanctuary, baptistry and tabernacle areas. It also proposed the development of the external wall to form a vertical overhanging garden with terracotta urns planted with trees; these proposals, however, were considered unsuitable for a church.

St Michael's Parish Church
Another commission, which was built, was to provide a new sanctuary which would conform to the teachings of Vatican II for St Michael's Parish Church in Inchicore, Dublin. Built in the nineteenth century as a military garrison church, it had been extended in the early twentieth century, and renovation—which originally proposed relocation of the sanctuary to the centre of the space, a plan considered too radical—called for the accentuation through natural light of the original sanctuary. This was achieved by introducing glazing and a circular drum over the space.

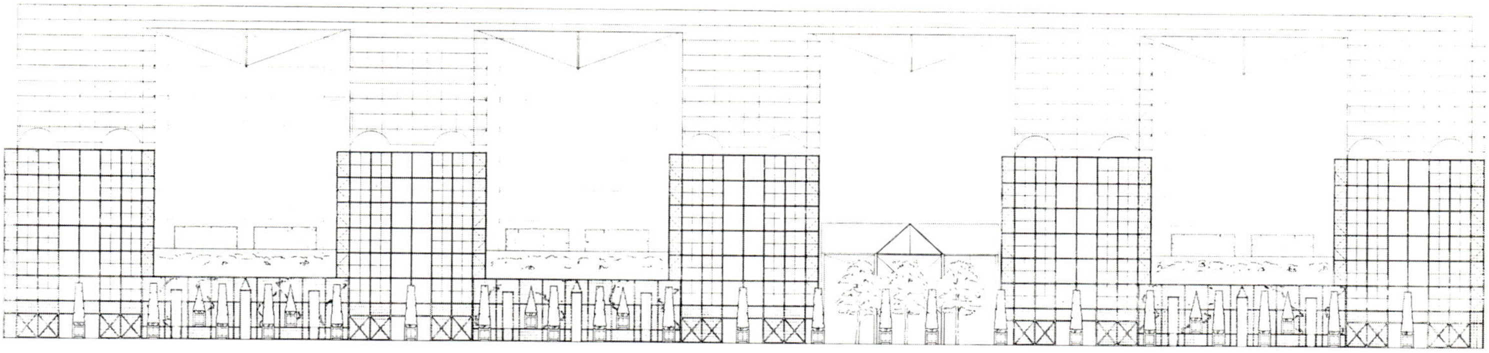

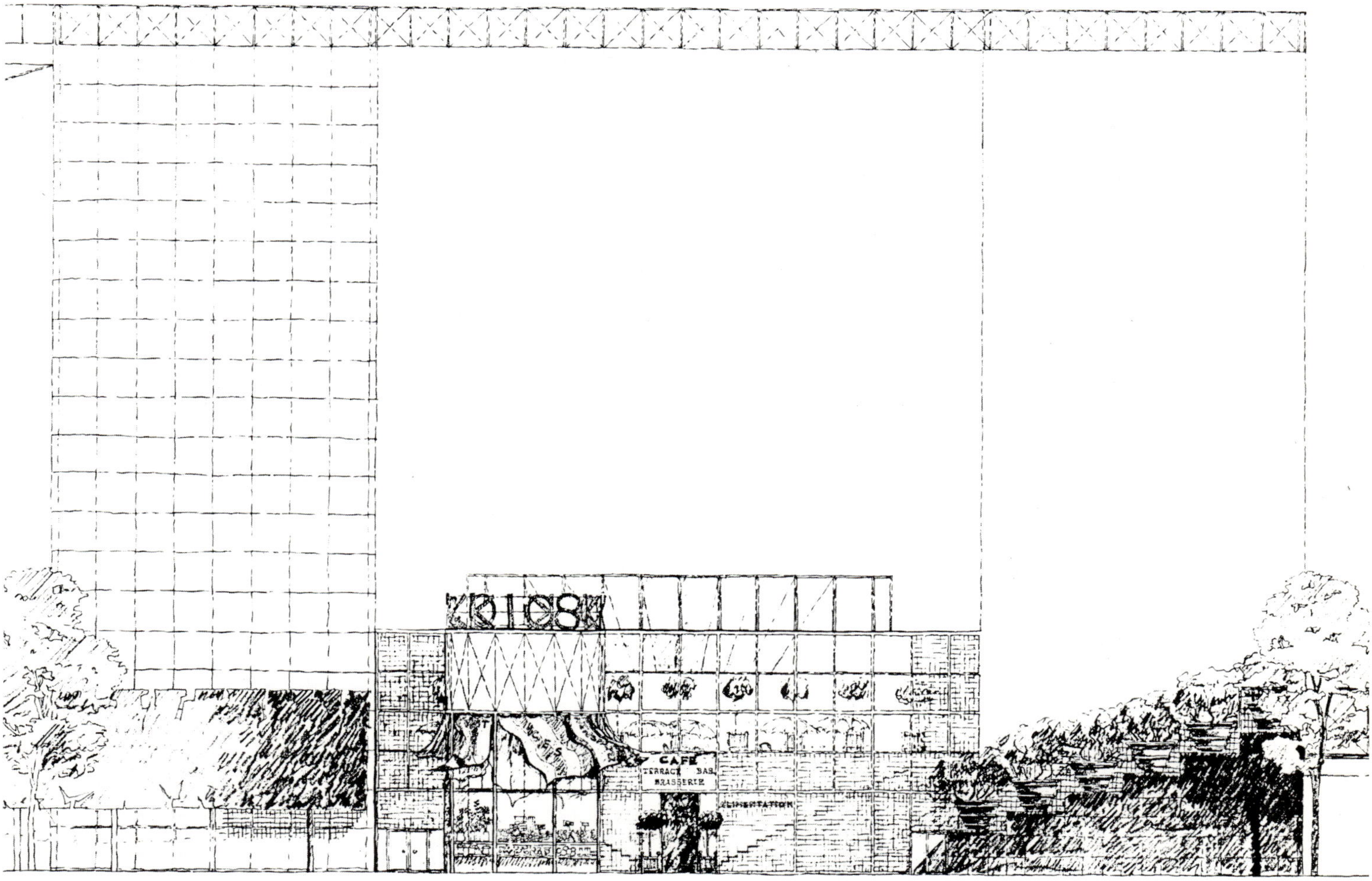

2, 3 EFFRA/EUROPEAN FERRIES COLD STORES SITE COMPETION, THAMES SIDE ELEVATION AND SHOPPING MALL.

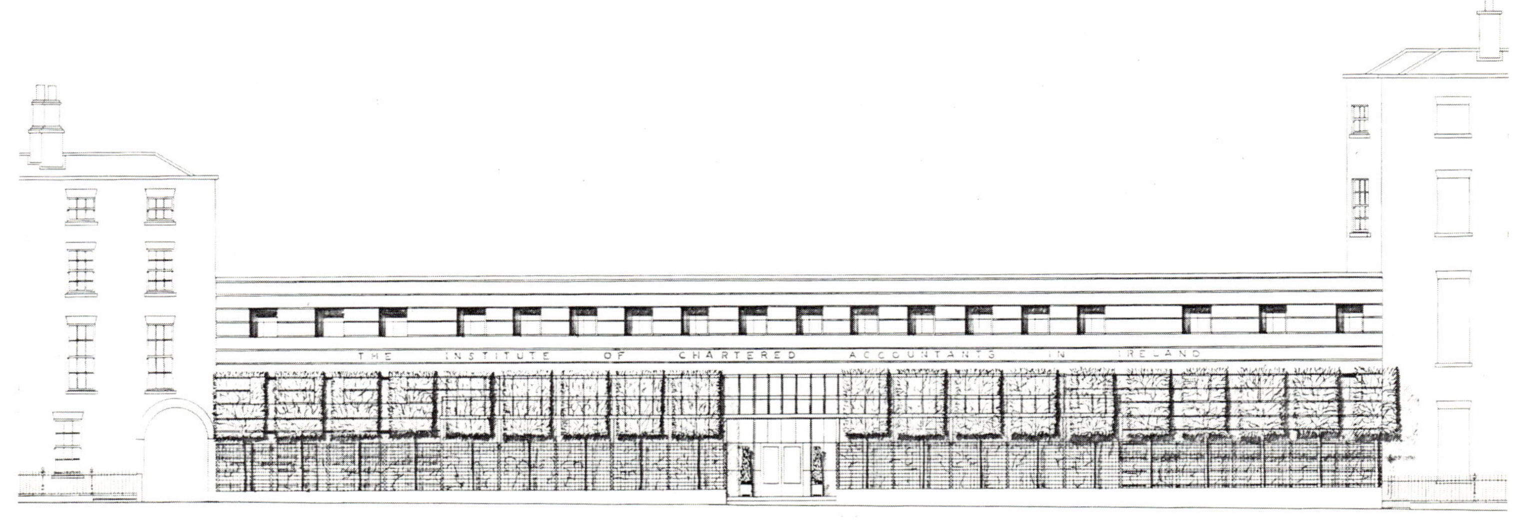

4 INSTITUTE OF CHARTERED ACCOUNTANTS IN IRELAND, STREET ELEVATION

5 SHELBOURNE HOTEL RESTORATION, ROOM 114.

6 ROWLAGH PARISH CHURCH, DUBLIN, EXTERIOR DETAIL.

7 ST MICHAEL'S PARISH CHURCH, INCHICORE, DUBLIN, ALTERATIONS.

MILTON KEYNES DEVELOPMENT CORPORATION
Housing Projects

1984 COMMENDATION

1 CENTRAL AREA INFILL 1.

Bradwell Common District
Located in central Milton Keynes, the project comprises forty houses of two- and three-storeys located along a main boulevard close to the city centre. The brief specifically called for a mix of houses for first time buyers who tend to prefer semi-detached housing, although this would have been at variance with the urban form that the city centre demands.

The design response to these conflicting parameters and the problem of the lack of identity inherent in most low-cost housing has been a specific grouping of buildings overlaid with a reoccuring theme of detail and colour. The three-storey pavilions define the boundaries of the site with the smaller dwellings located within courtyards.

ARCHITECTS Milton Keynes Development Cororation: K Revill, Building Director; P Moss, Divisional Architect; M Carter, Divisional Quantity Surveyor
PROJECT TEAM Gavin Hinton Cook, Jenny Phipps, Mike Smith
LANDSCAPE ARCHITECT Pat Green
COST PLANNER Jeremy Stacy

Downhead Park 5 Housing
The scheme (located in Fairford Crescent, Milton Keynes) comprises 76 dwellings arranged on a semi-circular site to provide a range of dwelling sizes from two-person flats to six-person family houses. The layout is symmetrical with three arcs of housing: the inner ring faces onto the local park where pairs of three-storey detached houses form a visual conclusion to the boulevard whilst the outer ring faces out onto the perimeter road. The middle ring is largely used to front onto the radiating pedestrian routes throughout the site.

ARCHITECTS AND CLIENT Milton Keynes Development Corporation
CONTRACTOR Robert Marriott Limited

Fishermead/Oldbrook Central Area Infill I
The brief proposed the residential development of three corner sites. Simple flats, based on a square plan, are stacked to three storeys whilst two-storey units make the transition in scale to the smaller adjacent residential developments. To the rear, low brick walls and open timber screens mark the transition between the scheme's public street frontage and the semi-private landscaped seating area beyond.

Housing for the elderly was also proposed: one and two bedroom single-storey dwellings are grouped around an internal pedestrian street. Each dwelling entrance and kitchen face onto this street, access to which is controlled to ensure security.

In designing both the flats and the dwellings for the elderly, the philosophy was the same: to open up the internal spaces of the small units to allow contact and mobility.

ARCHITECT Milton Keynes Development Corporation
CONTRACTOR Robert Marriot Limited

2-4 DOWNHEAD PARK 5, PLAN AND ELEVATIONS.

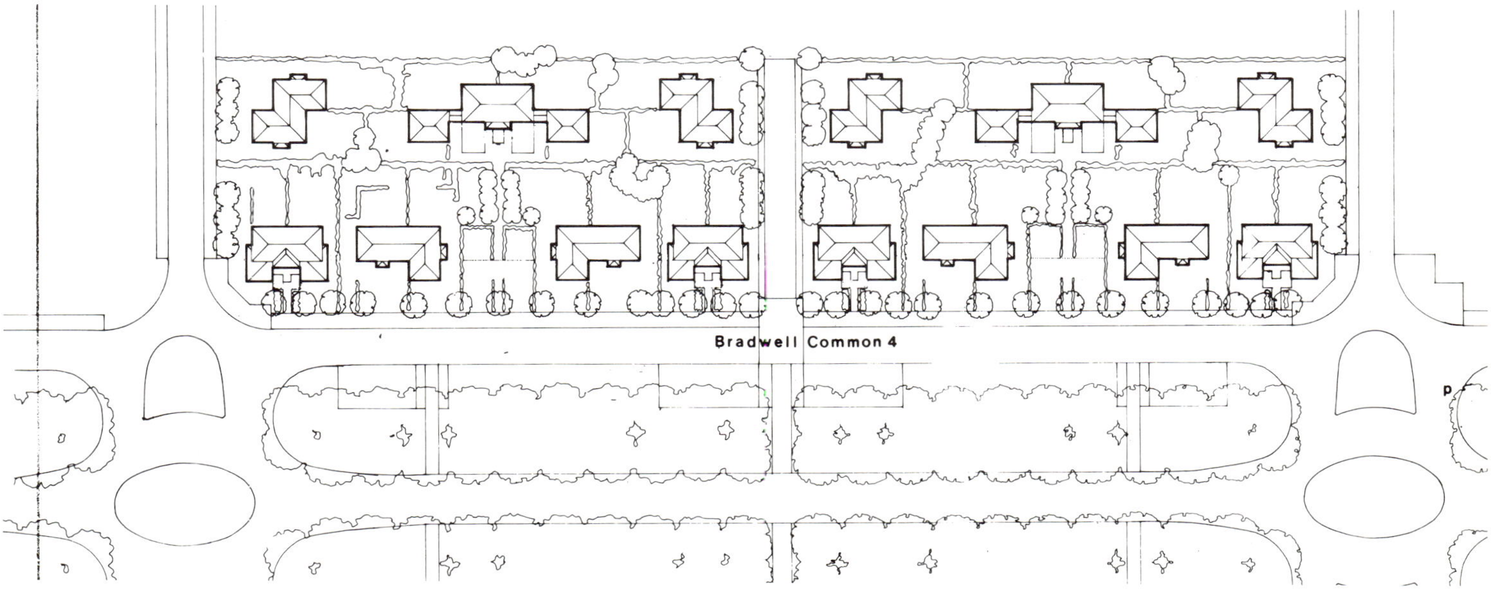

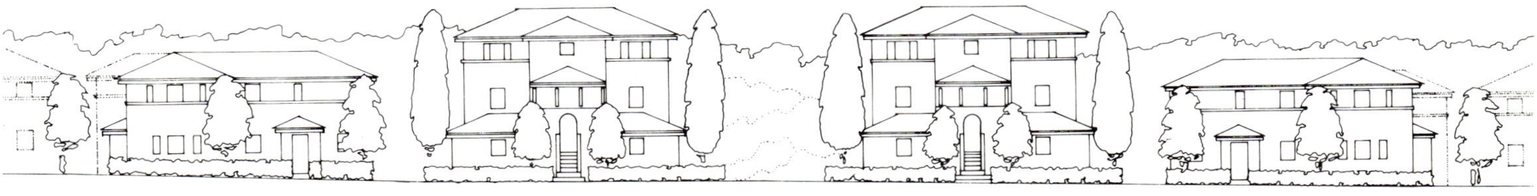

Bradwell Common 4

5-7 BRADWELL COMMON, THREE-STOREY PAVILION, STREET ELEVATION AND SITE LAYOUT.

PETER COOK, CHRISTINE HAWLEY & FS PLATOU A/S

Offices and Public Space, Oslo, 1984

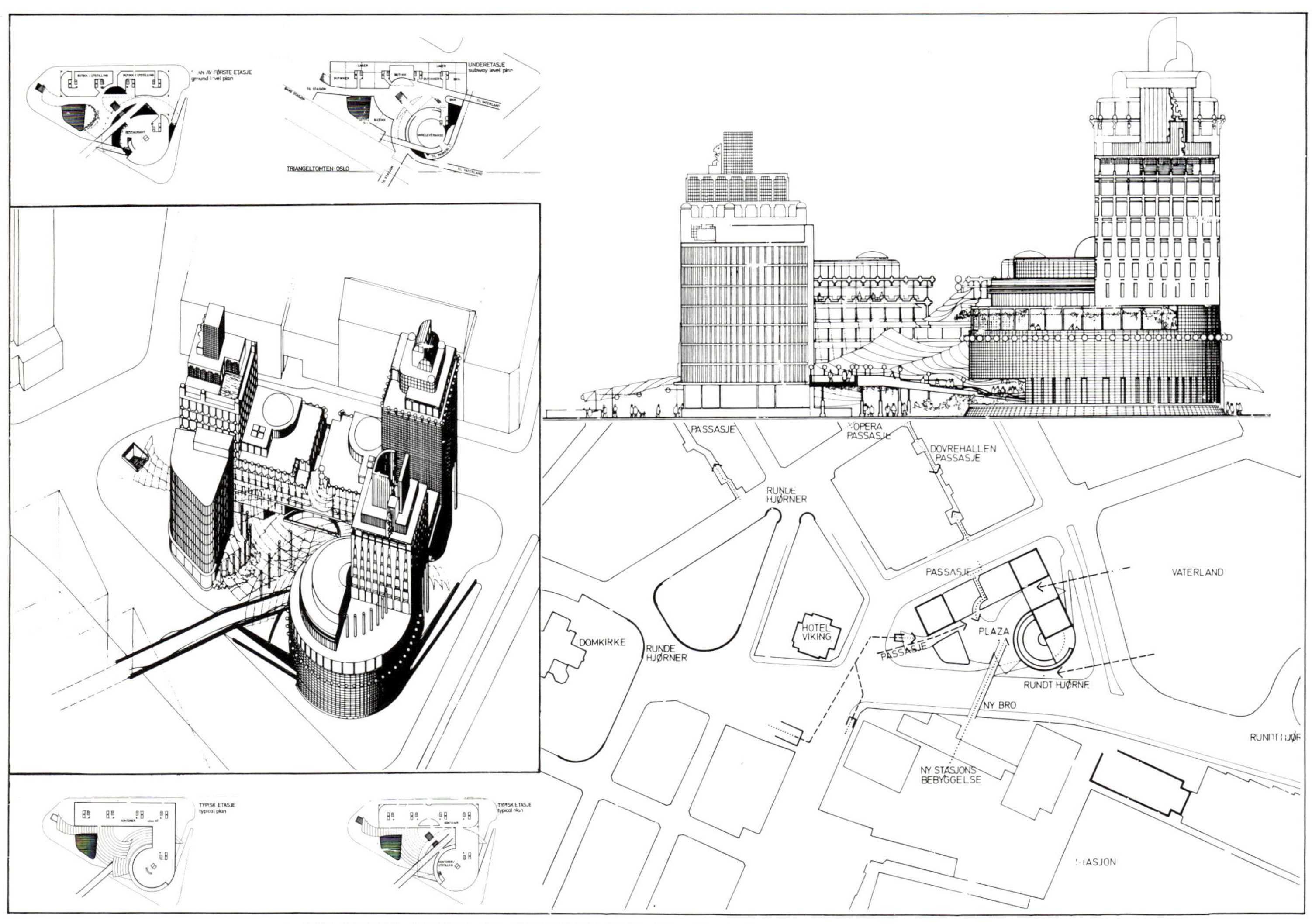

1 SITE, GROUND, SUBWAY AND TYPICAL FLOOR PLANS, AXONOMETRIC AND GUNNERUSGATE ELEVATION.

Site
Triangular site adjoining Oslo East Railway Station

Brief
To provide 35,000 square metres of office accommodation for Den Norske Creditbank A/S and their lessees, and to provide as much additional showroom and shopping accommodation as possible.

Interpretation
To pick up the character of the rounded cornered buildings in the district (by Erich Mendelsohnn and others), thereby creating a strong, dynamic architecture facing the main freeway to the south; to pick up the 'city' character to the north and north-west of the 5-6 storey buildings riddled with small alleys; to create a 'gate' to the old city centre to the west; to create another 'gate' to the new area of 'Vaterland' (subject of a recent competition); to create an office complex centring around gardens and an aviary, subdivided into office towers of identifiable character.

The later (coloured) elevations show the more recent work on the project where the surface of the building is treated as a series of layers. This is based upon orientation and considerations of winter light as well as patterns of identity to different internal uses within the towers and strips.

ARCHITECTS Peter Cook, Christine Hawley as consultant to F.S. Platou A/S Architects, Oslo
CLIENT Den Norske Creditbank A/S, Oslo

Architectural Design

Architectural Design has for many years been internationally acknowledged as foremost among a small number of specialist publications devoted to providing up-to-date information on architecture of both the present and past. Each issue, fully illustrated with drawings and often specially commissioned colour and black and white photographs, contains a thematic Profile which constitutes a detailed study, contributed by leading critics, historians or practitioners, of a contemporary architect, trend, building type or historical theme of current relevance, together with a magazine section consisting of letters, book reviews, theoretical articles and news of recent buildings, projects and competitions. The high standard of writing, editorial selection and presentation within *Architectural Design* has made it one of the world's leading architectural magazines, and essential reading for discerning architects and students alike.

AD has a policy of active participation in architectural discourse, and as well as commissioning special Profiles with the aim of furthering architectural debate on topical issues such as the role of classicism within contemporary practice, the magazine also sponsors lectures, competitions such as the increasingly influential annual Project Awards and the recent popular Dolls' House competition, to promote and stimulate architectural thinking and practice. *AD* subscribers are entitled to participate in any of the events organized by the magazine.

SUBSCRIBE NOW and read the magazine that leads the rest!

SUBSCRIPTION RATES

Full annual subscription
UK & Eire £39.50 Overseas US$75.00(£49.50)

Special annual student rate
UK & Eire £35.00 Overseas US$65.00(£42.50)

NOTE: Subscriptions can be backdated.

FREE GIFT. Every new subscriber using the 'Free Gift' card on the right will receive one of the following *AD* double issues/Profiles:

1. Surrealism
2. Roma Interrota
3. Neo-Classicism
4. Britain in the Thirties
5. Anglo-American Suburb
6. Viollet-le-Duc

To start your subscription now, please complete one of the cards on the right and send it with your payment/credit card authority/bank draft, direct to:-

Subscription Department,
ARCHITECTURAL DESIGN,
7/8 Holland Street,
London, W.8.

AD Profiles/back issues are available, please see overleaf for listing and order form.

ARCHITECTURAL DESIGN SUBSCRIPTION

☐ I wish to subscribe to *AD* at the full rate.
☐ I wish to subscribe to *AD* at the student rate, and enclose proof of student status.
(College .... Year ....)

Please circle the FREE GIFT of your choice:
1. Surrealism 2. Roma Interrota 3. Neo-Classicism
4. Britain in the Thirties 5. Anglo-American Suburb 6. Viollet-le-Duc

Starting date: Issue No .... Year ....
☐ Payment enclosed by: cheque/postal order/draft VALUE UK£/US$...........
☐ Please charge .... to my credit card.*
American Express - Diners Club - Access / Master Charge / Eurocard - Barclaycard / Visa
Account Number ....

Signature ....
Name ....
Address ....
....
....

* Credit cards will be charged in UK Sterling at current exchange rates.

Subscription Department,
ARCHITECTURAL DESIGN,
7/8 Holland Street,
London, W.8.

ARCHITECTURAL DESIGN SUBSCRIPTION

☐ I wish to subscribe to *AD* at the full rate.
☐ I wish to subscribe to *AD* at the student rate, and enclose proof of student status.
(College .... Year ....)

Please circle the FREE GIFT of your choice:
1. Surrealism 2. Roma Interrota 3. Neo-Classicism
4. Britain in the Thirties 5. Anglo-American Suburb 6. Viollet-le-Duc

Starting date: Issue No .... Year ....
☐ Payment enclosed by: cheque/postal order/draft VALUE UK£/US$...........
☐ Please charge .... to my credit card.*
American Express - Diners Club - Access / Master Charge / Eurocard - Barclaycard / Visa
Account Number ....

Signature ....
Name ....
Address ....
....
....

* Credit cards will be charged in UK Sterling at current exchange rates.

Subscription Department,
ARCHITECTURAL DESIGN,
7/8 Holland Street,
London, W.8.

AD PROFILES/BACK ISSUES

I wish to order the AD Profiles/back issues listed below:-

Issue	Cost	Issue	Cost
....	....	....	....
....	....	....	....
....	....	....	....
....	....	....	....

Please add £1.00/$2.00 per copy for postage and packing

☐ Payment enclosed by: cheque/postal order/draft VALUE UK£/US$...........

☐ Please charge .... to my credit card.*

American Express - Diners Club - Access/Master Charge/Eurocard -Barclaycard / Visa

Account Number ....

Signature.......................................

Name...

Address..

....

....

* Credit cards will be charged in UK Sterling at current exchange rates.

Subscription Department,
ARCHITECTURAL DESIGN,
7/8 Holland Street,
London, W.8.

AD PROFILES/BACK ISSUES

***AD* Profiles/back issues available as listed below. To order please complete card on left adding £1.00/$2.00 per copy for postage and packing.**

1977

1	Arata Isozaki	£2.95/$5.95
3	Tafuri-Culot-Krier	£2.95/$5.95
4	Post-Modernism	£2.95/$5.95
7	Millbank	£2.95/$5.95

1978

10	Post-Modern History	£2.95/$5.95
11	Surrealism	£4.95/$9.95
14	Handbuilt Hornby	£2.95/$5.95
15	France + map guide to Paris	£4.95/$9.95
16	Bruce Goff	£4.95/$9.95
17	Beaux-Arts + map guide	£4.95/$9.95

1979

19	Sainsbury Centre	£2.95/$5.95
20	Roma Interrotta + map guide	£4.95/$9.95
21	Leon Battista Alberti	£4.95/$9.95
22	Christchurch Spitalfields	£2.95/$5.95
23	Neo-Classicism	£4.95/$9.95
24	Britain in the Thirties + map guide	£4.95/$9.95
25	Aalto and After	£3.95/$7.95

1980

26	New Free Style	£4.95/$9.95
27	Viollet-le-Duc	£4.95/$9.95
28	Post-Modern Classicism	£7.50/$14.95
29	Stirling Gold	£4.95/$9.95
30	Les Halles	£4.95/$9.95
31	Urbanity	£4.95/$9.95

1981

32	Futurism & Rationalism	£4.95/$9.95
33	British Architects	£4.95/$9.95
34	Romantic Houses	£3.95/$7.95
35	Methodology of Arch. History	£7.50/$14.95
37	Anglo-American Suburb	£4.95/$9.95
38	Current Projects	£3.95/$7.95

1982

39	Free Style Classicism	£7.50/$14.95
41	Classicism is not a Style	£7.50/$14.95
42	Modern Architecture	£7.50/$14.95
43	Animated Architecture	£7.50/$14.95
44	Forest Edge/Post-War Berlin	£7.50/$14.95

1983

45	Architecture in Progress – IBA	£7.50/$14.95
46	Dolls' Houses	£9.95/$19.95
47	Russian Avant-Garde	£7.50/$14.95
48	Abstract Representation	£7.50/$14.95
49	Elements of Architecture	£7.50/$14.95
50	Berlin History	£7.50/$14.95

1984

51	Urbanism	£7.50/$14.95
52	Rationalism	£7.50/$14.95
53	British Architecture	£7.50/$14.95
54	Leon Krier	£7.50/$14.95

AD Special Profiles

Quinlan Terry	£4.95/$9.95
Robert Stern	£7.50/$14.95
Bernard Tschumi	£4.95/$9.95
Los Angeles I + II	£12.50/$24.95
James Stirling	£7.50/$14.95

AD Special Issues

British Architecture	£14.95/$29.50
AD Subscriber's Price	£9.95/$19.95
+ postage and packing	£2.00/$4.00

UK in Sterling /Overseas in US$

TRIANGELTOMTEN·OSLO FASADE TIL VATERLAND PETER COOK / F.S PLATOU 1982

2 'VATERLAND' FACADE.

3 NORTH FACADE.

DEREK WALKER ASSOCIATES

Story Village, 1984

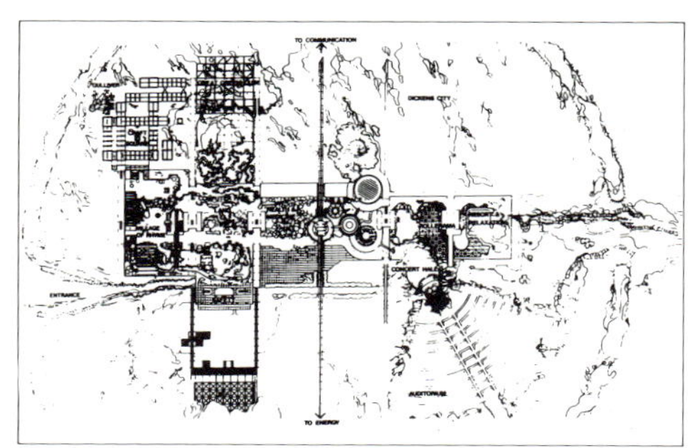

1 SITE PLAN.

Story Village is a vast toy box assembly, under a high overhead crystalline canopy, of many of the images, artifacts and characters of English childhood. On a cascading series of levels following the slope of the man-made canyon (on which the theme building itself is sited), every trick and strategem of scale, enclosure, level, colour and light has been used to create a world outside space and time, familiar but impossible, peopled with well-remembered characters such as Jack Spratt and his wife, Little Bo-Peep, the cow, the moon, the dish and the spoon.

The journey begins at entrance concourse level, the lowest of five levels in the theme building. From here (the beginning of a story) the Village is entered through a giant pop-up book, one among a pile of books which appears to have fallen in an untidy heap at the Village entrance. One may ascend to the lower concourse by escalator (past the luminous crystal chapel) or by a series of rock-hewn stairways, past the entrance to Alan Aldridge's Butterfly Ball ride to the Village Square. At the top of the rocky steps, against the flank wall of the Rhyme Time Theatre is another bewildering trick of scale, a giant pile of forgotten childrens' toys, puppets, dice, chessmen, tops, some thirty feet in height and brightly coloured.

Through to the Village Square: the Rhyme Time Theatre presents an elegant classical facade to the square which on closer inspection turns out to be a series of plywood thin stage-sets. Other sides to the square, mainly restaurants and shops, are equally fantastic—part giant child's construction kit, part scaled-up bedroom furniture, part gingerbread/post-modern eclecticism. In the centre of the square is a tea pot, twice as high as a man: on the right, the Rev Awdreys Red Engine Ride, complete with murmuring engines, which disappear into a tunnel and take passengers the full circuit of the Village.

Up out of the Village Square past the giant shoe (entrance to the Shoehouse Ride) and tree-house to Market Square at upper Concourse level: on the right is a battlemented castle-keep with drawbridge and ahead, a giant doll's house with doors half-open, the entrance to the Father Christmas ride.

Past the Rhyme-Time restaurant one is outside the theme building in the Craft Square. This is a two-storey enclosure built, apparently, of a giant's Meccano kit and containing an assembly of craft shops, workshops, a dairy and an animal enclosure.

On the opposite side of the Crafts Square, 20 feet high but thankfully on his back and tethered securely to the ground, lies Gulliver, the climax of the journey.

Other Story Village structures and rides include: The Rev Awdry's Railway; The Butterfly Ball; The Rhyme Time Theatre; The Shoe House ride; The Father Christmas ride; The Crooked House; The Village Square; The Village Square Bandstand; The Teapot Store and Tearoom; The Clocktower Tearoom; Jack Spratt's Restaurant; The Rhyme Time Restaurant; The Village Bakery; The Castle Restaurant; The Pumpkin Restaurant; The Baby Shop; The Village Bookshop; The Toyshop; The Theatre Sweet Shop; The Village Flowershop; Mother Hubbard's Cupboard Store; The Market Hall; The Village Emporium; The Station Kiosk; Dickory Dock's Clock Tower; The Doll's House Shop; The Market Hall kiosk; The Market Square; The Tree House; The Castle Playground; The Village Church.

CLIENTS Group 5
ARCHITECTS Derek Walker Associates
DESIGN TEAM Group 5, G Baptist, I Quicke, DWA: K Hines, S Horne, G Reofern, D Walker
MODELMAKER I Dowsett
PHOTOGRAPHER K Kirkwoto

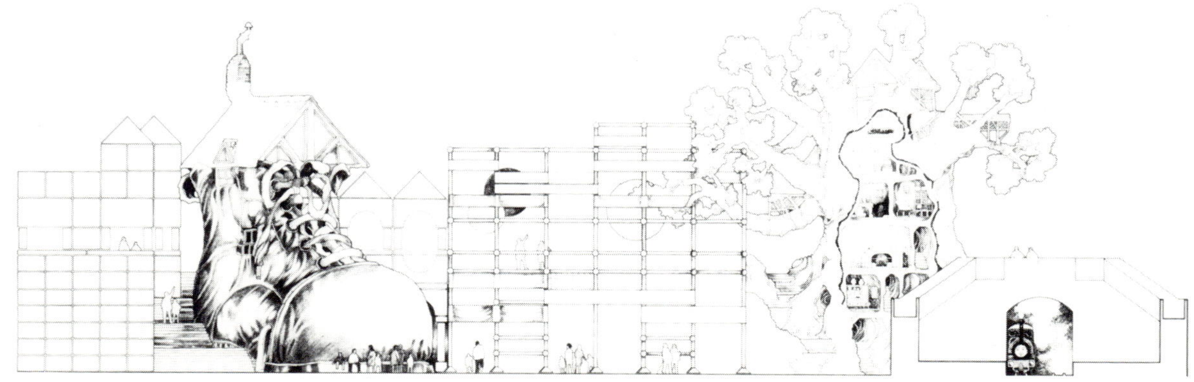

2 VILLAGE SQUARE ELEVATION.

3 AXONOMETRIC.

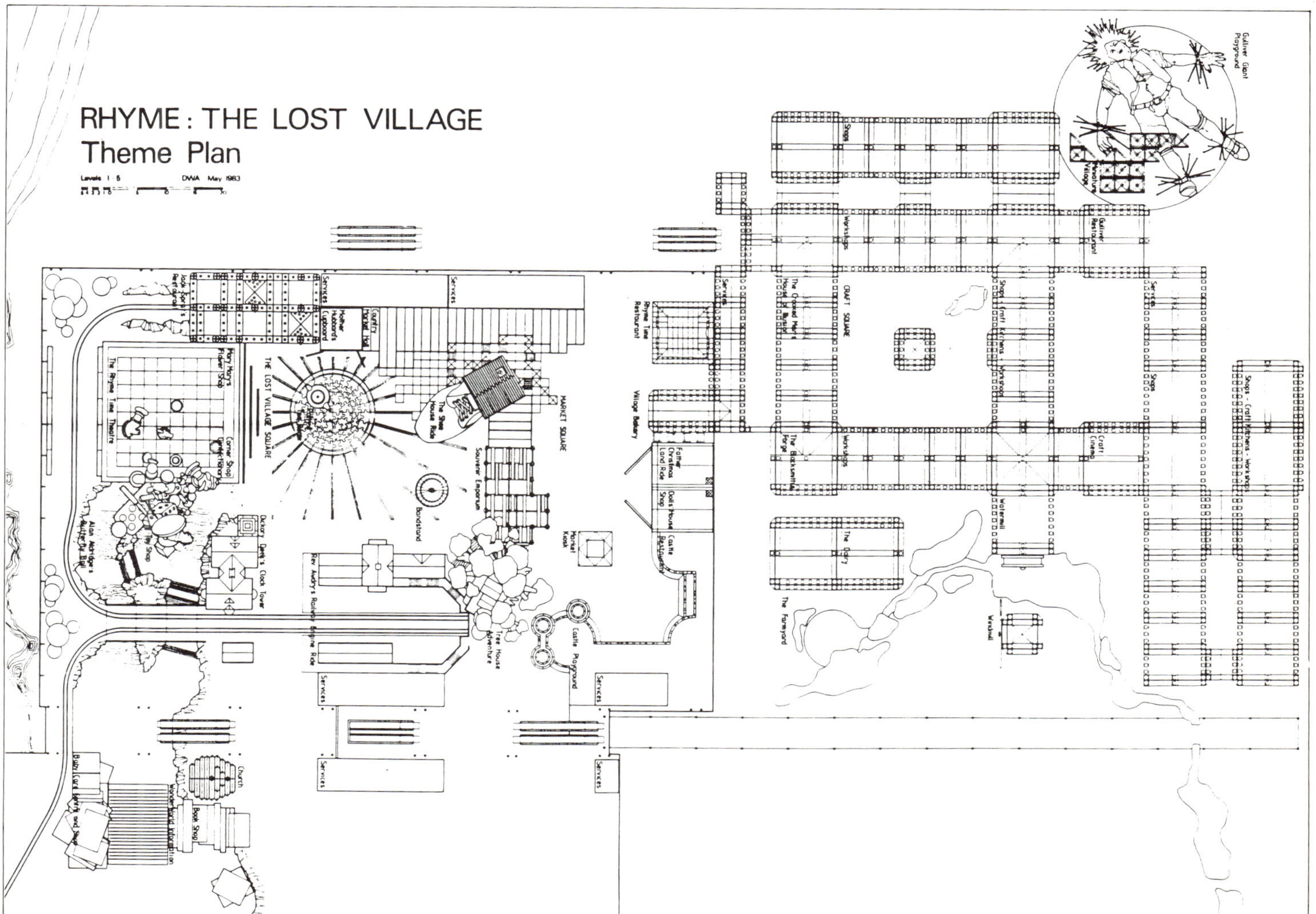

RHYME: THE LOST VILLAGE
Theme Plan

4 THEME PLAN.

5 JACK SPRATT RESTAURANT.

6 RHYME TIME THEATRE.

7 LOWER VILLAGE SQUARE.

8 GENERAL VIEW OF VILLAGE. (PHS K KIRKWOTO)

COLQUHOUN + MILLER
Whitechapel Art Gallery, London 1982-5
1984 AWARD

1 PERSPECTIVE OF RECEPTION AREA.

The Whitechapel Art Gallery originally designed by C Harrison Townsend in 1899 is a Listed Building Grade II, and in particular the facade is one of the few notable examples of the Art Nouveau style in England.

There were two major constraints concerned with preservation. First, Townsend's facade could not be altered (except to remove two attic windows inserted into what was to have been a mosaic frieze). Second, the client and the Greater London Council wanted the main galleries to be left intact as far as possible.

Based on an initial list of requirements, the actual new accommodation and its distribution was laboriously worked out in collaboration with the client to achieve the best solution in the face of spatial and budgetary constrictions. Almost every relocation of one programmatic element entailed a complete change in overall distribution, and this process took a very long time before a solution was found which was satisfactory both to the client and to the architects.

The new accommodation required was broadly as follows: extra gallery space; extra office space; extra storage, loading facilities, and preparation spaces and a goods lift; new lecture and education spaces, and a larger cafeteria, all of which could be used independently to the Gallery; alternative access to each gallery level, so that one could be used while the other was being prepared for a new exhibition; new book store; extra space for mechanical and electrical services and ductwork: changes in lighting and sun control (all which were required to be discrete, and subordinate to the original structural profiles).

These new elements had to be provided either within the existing building envelope, or in a new extension occupying a narrow strip of land in Angel Alley. Investigation proved that the existing school building (1870) in the alley could not be economically adapted to the new uses, and it was decided to demolish it and erect a new five-storey structure, sharing a long party wall with the existing gallery.

The most important internal alterations affecting the public use of the two existing galleries are the two new staircases. One provides a visually apparent public access to the first floor gallery from the foyer. The other, a long continuous flight broken only by a lobby to the cafeteria, leads to the far end of the upper gallery via a new gallery on the first floor. Both staircases replace existing ones enclosed in a brick structure.

The existing interiors are stylistically neutral—the bare statement of an industrial basilica space reminiscent of nineteenth-century market structures. There are few clues as to the treatment of new elements, though certain motifs, such as roof lighting to the gallery and the entrance arch, have been reinforced. The old gallery spaces have been preserved except for the replacement of the enclosed staircase at the far end by an open one. Both new staircases provide what was lacking in the original building: a sense of spatial continuity between the ground floor and first floor galleries. Thus, the typical spaces have been maintained, while the linking spaces between and outside them have been completely transformed. Interstitial areas of transition have been created and dramatised where none existed previously. These areas have been treated as new inventions, adding to the old building something that was never envisaged when it was built.

The new facade on Angel Alley is not visible from the main road and can never be seen at the same time as Townsend's facade. The new facade has also been treated freely, with only oblique references to the plastic movement and string courses of the Art Nouveau frontispiece. The concave wall to the cafeteria presses against the narrow space of the alley. The relative elaboration of this rather secret facade is deliberate; it will be discovered by chance, announcing the presence of the gallery, whose interior nave is carved out of the brick fabric of east London.

A solution that depends so much on the accidents of the site and the special demands of the programme can hardly be offered as typical of the problem of adding to existing buildings. Yet there are features which may go beyond the particular case. Firstly, the skeletal and reduced quality of the existing gallery spaces seems to have a morphological typicality about it which encourages its preservation, but at the same time presents no stylistic constraint on what may be added. Secondly, since Townsend's elaborate facade recalls the architectural tradition in a way that has already been transformed by an idiosyncratic will, and in the spirit of the avant-garde, it seems positively to encourage further transformation. Our strategy in modifying this building has therefore been based, on the one hand, on the need to preserve all that is typical, and, on the other, on the licence to invent new forms and not in any way to copy the particular clothing that the type was given in the first instance. What is new comes just as much from a moment in history as did Townsend's original.

ARCHITECTS Colquhoun + Miller
SERVICES ENGINEERS Steenson Varming Mulcahy & Partners
QUANTITY SURVEYORS Brian Davis Associates
STRUCTURAL ENGINEERS F J Samuely & Partners

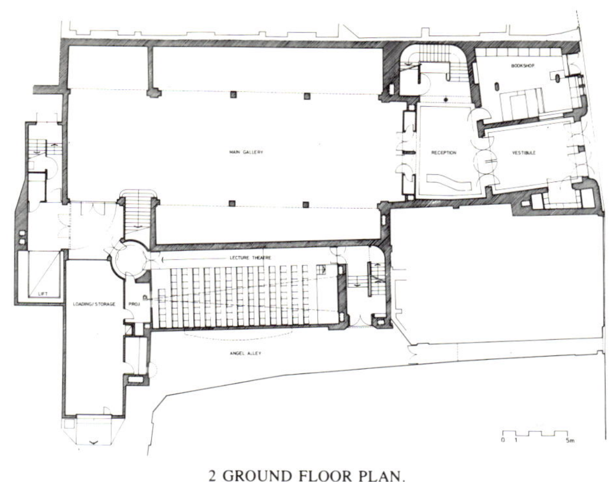

2 GROUND FLOOR PLAN.

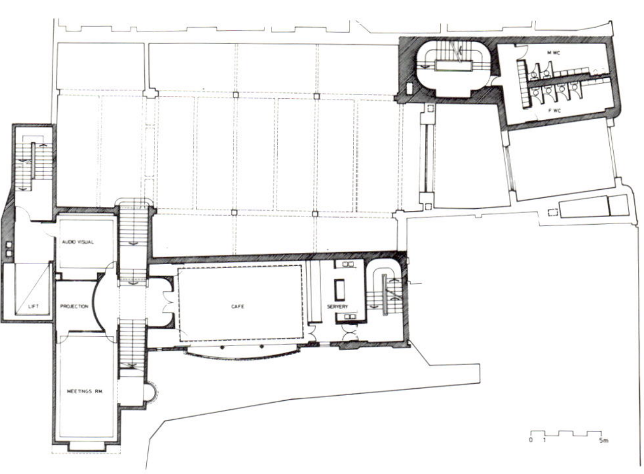

3 MEZZANINE PLAN.

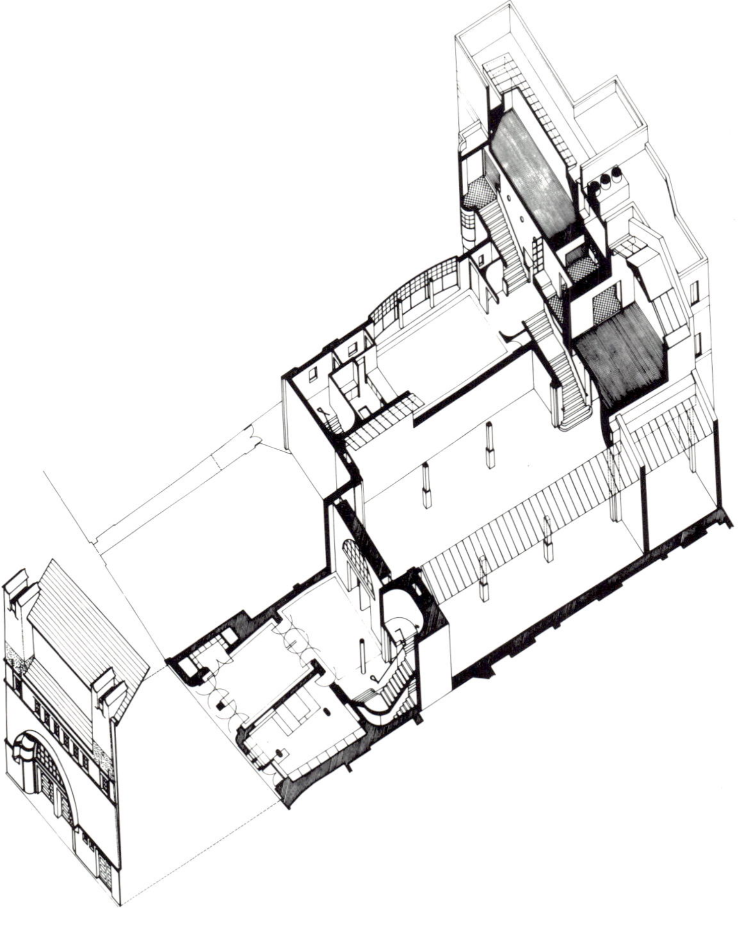

4 CUTAWAY AXONOMETRIC.

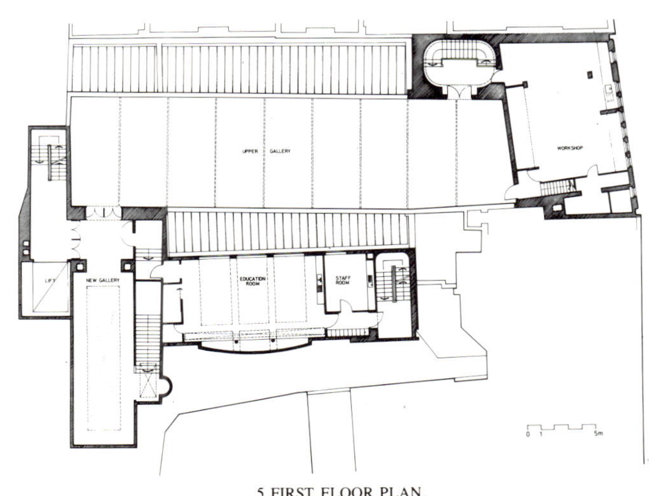

5 FIRST FLOOR PLAN.

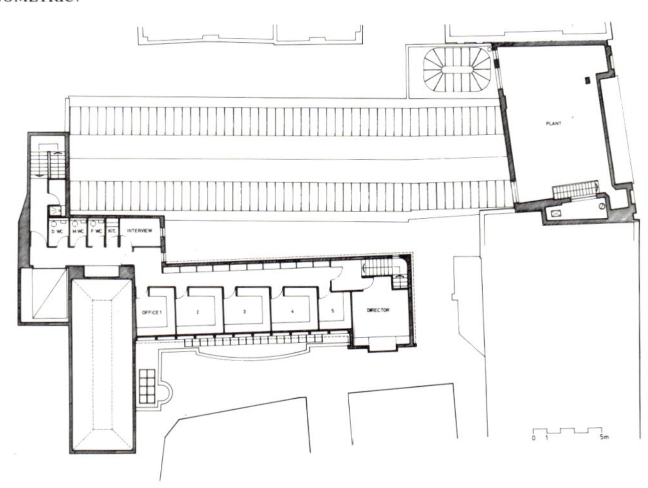

6 SECOND FLOOR PLAN.

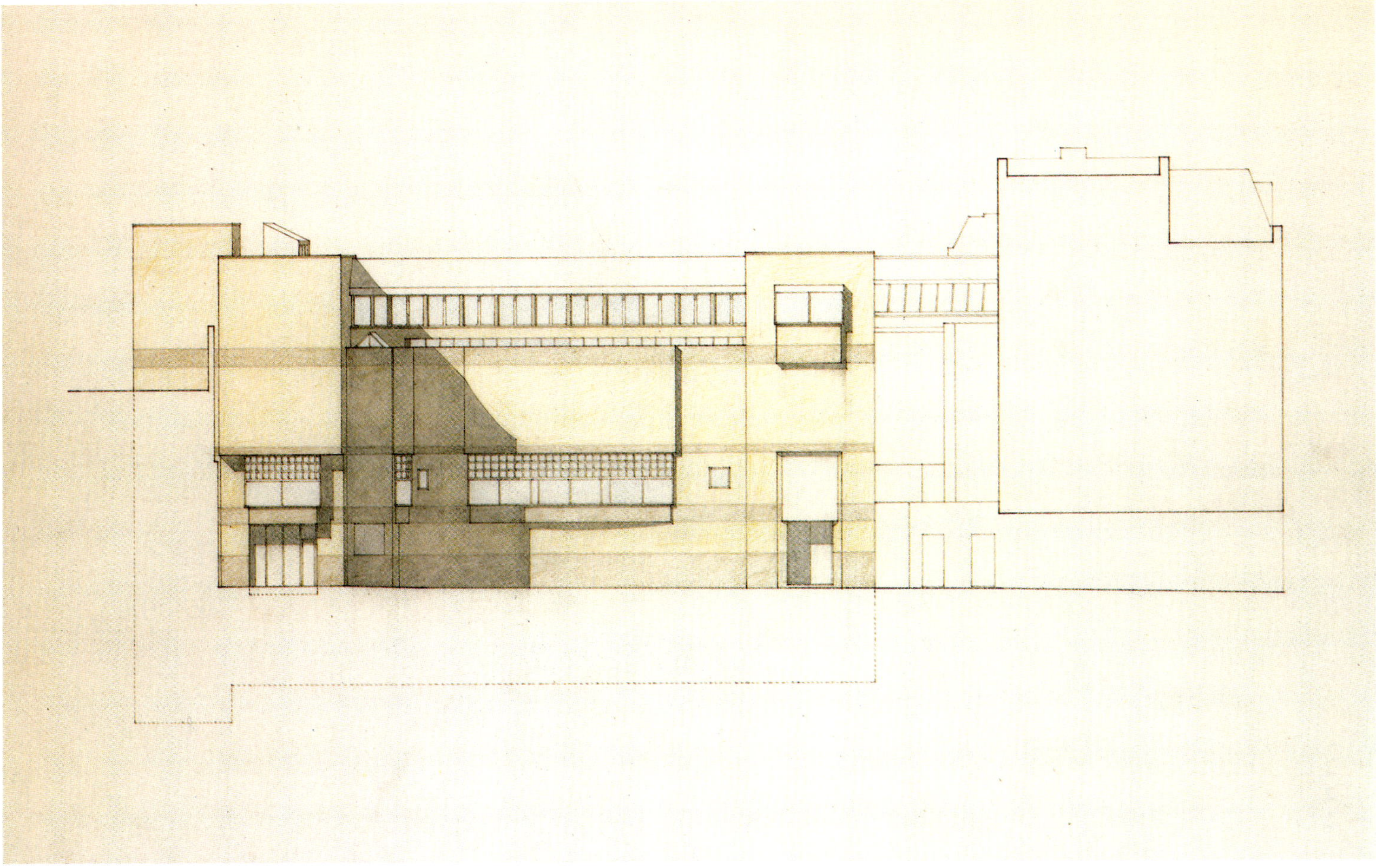

7 WEST ELEVATION

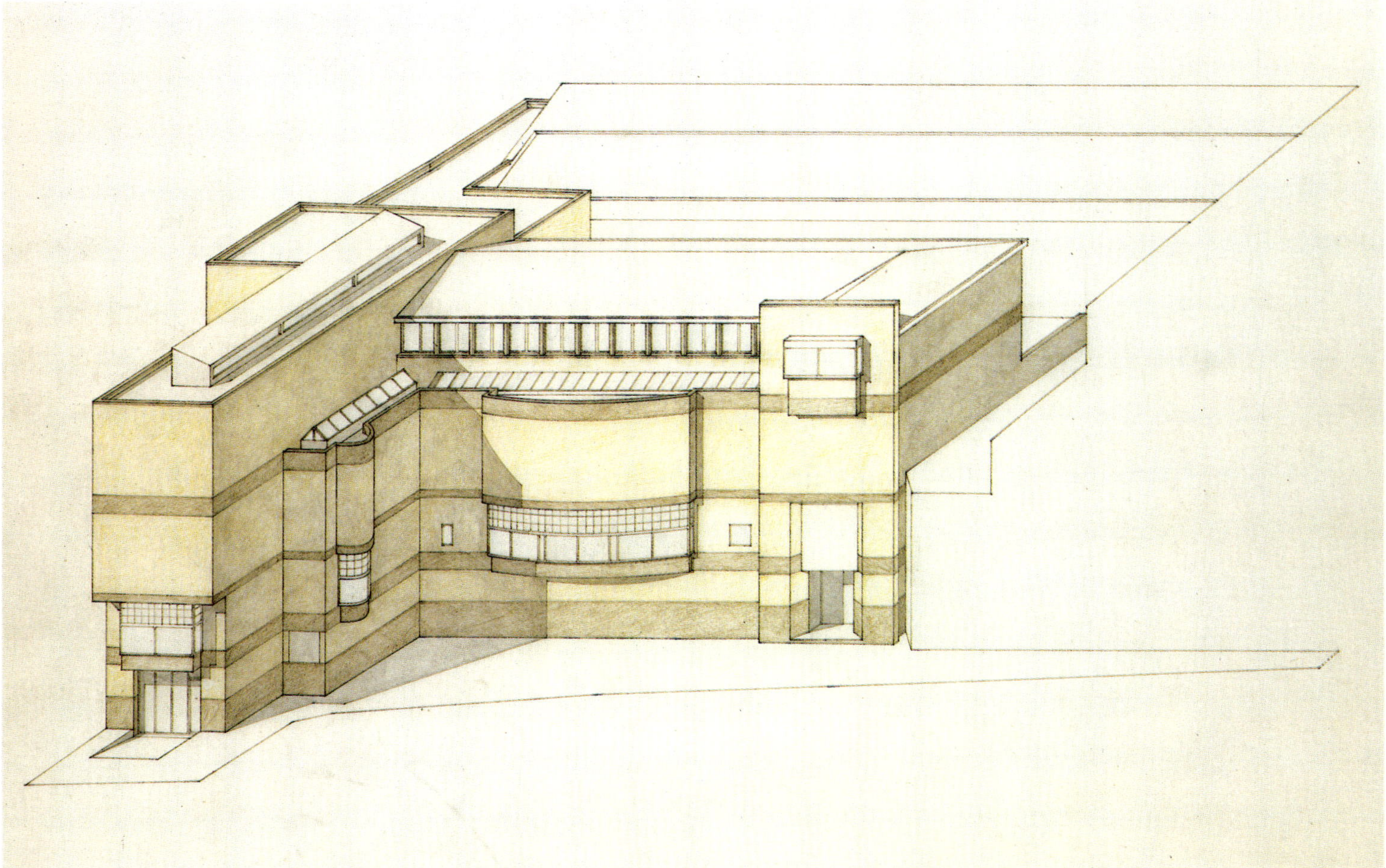

8 ISOMETRIC FROM ANGEL ALLEY.

NICHOLAS GRIMSHAW & PARTNERS

Warehouse and Distribution Centre for Herman Miller, Chippenham 1983

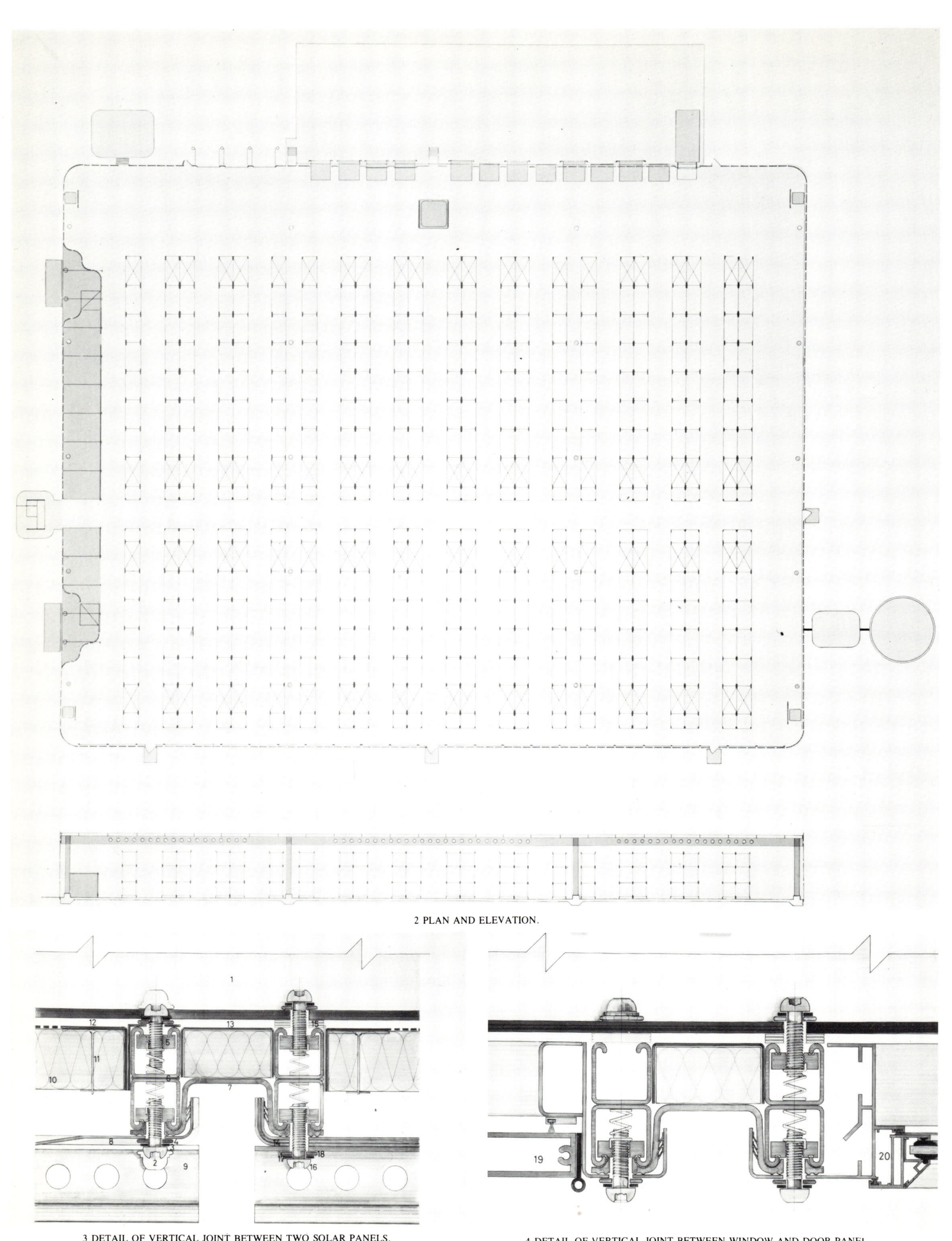

2 PLAN AND ELEVATION.

3 DETAIL OF VERTICAL JOINT BETWEEN TWO SOLAR PANELS.

4 DETAIL OF VERTICAL JOINT BETWEEN WINDOW AND DOOR PANEL. (PHS GRAHAM NASH LTD)

5 INTERIOR (PH JO REID & JOHN PECK)

The 14-acre site is owned by Herman Miller and has outline planning permission for 240,000 sq ft of industrial building. Phase I occupies approximately one-third of its full potential. After testing several alternatives the architects discovered a strange anomaly: namely that, although the site's boundaries are totally irregular, the best way to maximise the total building area as a single rectangle was to design the estate road as a ring in the form of a perfect ellipse. The elliptical shape will become more evident after the completion of Phases II and III.

Seen as the first building in Chippenham by drivers along the A4 and railway passengers along the embankment (three million a year according to British Rail), this warehouse was designed to offer the public a dramatic and easily memorable image of elegant modern technology in strong contrast with its landscape setting. Earlier schemes (discarded owing to the conservatism of funding institutions) would have achieved this by placing the structure on the outside. The current scheme tries to achieve the same effect through its colour and the high degree of modelling in its cladding.

RSJs 919mm-deep span continuously over 400mm diameter tubular columns giving one central span of 36 metres and two side ones of 28.8 metres. Together with the 6.581 metres clear internal height, this gives considerable racking flexibility. The beams were delivered in sections and site welded in place using temporary propping. Each weld was independently tested by specialists. Steel plate cut from the beam webs to form the circular holes (which reduce their self-weight) can be found in the form of fixed seats in the external relaxing area.

The roof has no falls or valley gutters. Instead, rainwater drains away into outlets positioned at midspan as the structure and decking deflect under its accumulating weight. The waterproof membrane comprises a single skin of proprietory PVC sheet solvent welded together and to small circular PVC discs screwed through the insulation into the steel roof deck.

The cladding was conceived on an identical principal to the Herman Miller action office programme: namely that of an interchangeable kit of parts.

Solid panels, fixed windows, opening windows, fire doors, and personnel doors may all be unbolted and moved to any location on a 2.4 x 1.2 metre grid. The four apertures of each window frame allow the further flexibility of interchanging glass with a vocabulary of secondary components such as external lights, ventilation louvres and components allowing pipe transitions.

Technically this was achieved by using doubled pairs of unistrut channels (which allow bolted fixings anywhere along their length) with continuous black strips of a special neoprene extrusion slotted between each pair providing the weather seal at each vertical panel joint. Horizontally each higher panel laps over each lower one and each joint is stiffened by a special 'T' bar (this doubles up as a ladder rail). Internally, insulation and sound absorption are achieved by separate perforated steel liner trays and Rockwool slabs. All external components are Syntha Pulvin coated aluminium, apart from the bolts which are stainless steel.

This Warehouse was erected between July 1982 and April 1983 for £1,689,000. A floor area of 75,000 sq ft gives it a cost of £22.5 per sq. ft.

ARCHITECTS Nicholas Grimshaw & Partners; Partner, Brian Taggart; Senior Architect, David Richmond; Assistant Architect, Alan Robshaw
DESIGN TEAM Partner-in-charge—Nicholas Grimshaw; Project architects—Nevan Sidor, Ian McArdle, Mark Goldstein
CLIENT Herman Miller Limited
STRUCTURAL ENGINEERS Peter Brett Associates
SERVICES ENGINEERS YRM Engineers
QUANTITY SURVEYORS Gardiner & Theobald
LANDSCAPE ARCHITECTS Thames Landscape Group
GENERAL CONTRACTOR Wimpey Construction (UK) Ltd

ARUP ASSOCIATES
Liverpool Garden Festival Building, 1984

1 DETAIL OF DOME.

The Festival Hall was the winning entry of a single-stage architectural competition, one of those set up on the initiative of the then Environmental Secretary, Michael Heseltine, and was the first to be completed. The results were published in May 1982 and the building had to be completed by February 1984, after 12 months on site.

The competition was held to choose a design for a hall which would later be converted into a regional sports centre. A detailed brief was written for each use and it was necessary to consider the marriage of the two in considerable detail. There was no guarantee, however, that the sports conversion would ever be carried out.

The Garden Festival Hall is the first major building to be realised by the Merseyside Development Corporation, and is therefore not only a central focus to the Garden Festival but is also seen as a symbol of regeneration on Merseyside. A festival is a celebration and consequently its main building should reflect this mood. The festival building, like a theatre, is a shell within which the widest possible range of events can be mounted. Its design was intended to carefully balance with the scale of its surroundings and to have a simplicity and immediacy which everyone can understand.

The festival needs a very strong statement at its centre; the hall must act as a backdrop to exhibits of the smallest scale and should feel welcoming.

In this building the form is the structure, and the weathering envelope is composed of two related forms: the dome and the vault. The dome is halved and then rejoined by the linear vault. The structural and economic efficiency derived from this curvilinear form results in low material content and a favourable ratio between surface and plan area. Furthermore, the removal of the differentiation between wall and roof reduced the number of materials and their detailing to a minimum.

The building is designed with the following main aims:

- to be recessive when viewed within the landscape but to be exaggerated in its scale, size and excitement when it is entered;
- to form one envelope which unifies the building and yet defines and expresses the three principal activity areas of the exhibition and its division into pool, hall and club after conversion;
- to provide a 7500 square metre column-free enclosure to give maximum flexibility for both the festival and the sports complex;
- to form an external surface requiring little maintenance.

The envelope is energy-efficient and low on maintenance costs. The long, low dome structures are clad in profiled aluminium sheet which has a composite insulating base to provide a high level of heat insulation, acoustic treatment and a vapour barrier to withstand the high humidity levels in a leisure pool. The central transparent vault is covered in 20mm polycarbonate sheet treated to combat glare by refraction within its cellular structure. This gives an environment which is suitable for plants, but will also provide an area suitable for sports. The reflective 'glassy' finish of the polycarbonate provides an appropriate sparkle to the garden with its strong association with the great glass structures of Paxton and Decimus Burton, but when viewed at a distance against the garden exhibits themselves, it sits quietly as a backdrop.

The building was handed over to the festival organisers in February 1984.

ARCHITECTS, ENGINEERS, AND QUANTITY SURVEYORS Arup Associates
CLIENT Merseyside Development Corporation
STRUCTURAL STEELWORK Tubeworkers Ltd
ELECTRICAL INSTALLATION How Group Northern Ltd
CONTRACTOR Norwest Holst Projects Limited

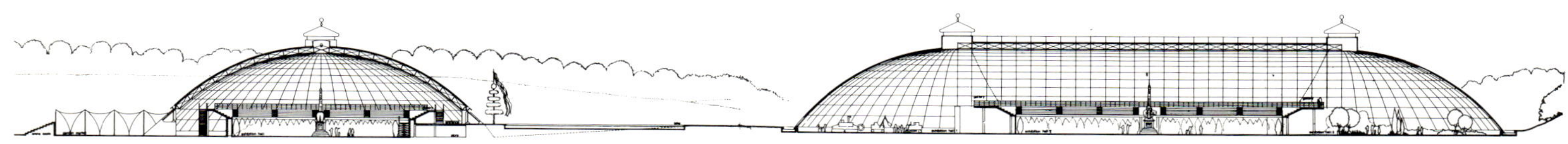

2 SECTIONS TOWARDS RIVER AND ARENA.

3 DETAIL OF VAULT.

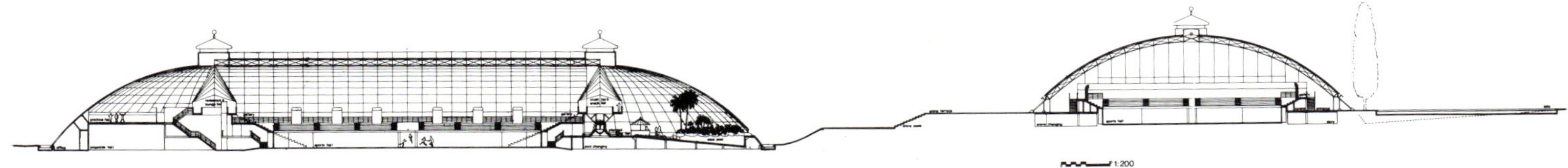

4 SECTIONS TOWARDS ARENA AND RIVER.

CAMPBELL, ZOGOLOVITCH, WILKINSON & GOUGH ARCHITECTS

China Wharf, Mill Street, London

1984 COMMENDATION

1 PERSPECTIVE FROM THE RIVER.

China Wharf is a block of seventeen flats with offices on the ground and part first floors on the Thames at Bermondsey. To pack them in with living rooms all facing the river and the bedrooms behind without external access, the flats are designed in a scissors arrangement.

China Wharf has three mannerist facades. The Mill Street elevation is the closest in style to its ex-warehouse neighbours. The window openings in the brickwork reduce in size towards the centre loophole frame opening. This false perspective effect partly emphasises the openings' size and partly graduates between the different windows of the neighbouring buildings; it satisfactorily expresses the transition from bedroom to bathroom inside. The loophole opening itself is an elongated keystone to the entrance arch (or half-arch) on the ground floor and expresses the circulation area of the building, the loophole being the hoisting circulation of a warehouse. This circulation area of lift and stairs is shared by the existing Reeds Wharf next door and this unusual relationship is shown in the way that the building appears to run right into the opening. The sky sign at the top operates in the street to denote the entrance facade and in the traditional way downriver to approaching boats.

The image of the courtyard is an inside-out silo. It looks at first like an industrial building but its form would be really useless unless it were the imprint of a pre-existing silo in the courtyard space. The reason for the shape is a desire to turn these bedroom windows away from direct overlooking views across the courtyard without recourse to a student hostel saw-tooth. The form has been read as the base of a giant Ionic pilaster. However, the idea of the sleeping quarters of a residential block being thought of as a silo is more seductive.

The ground storey is separately expressed with a setback of part support and part funnel down to giant short columns. The courtyard continues under the building's excessive implied weight to create parking space.

The relationship between these two elevations is ambivalent. The pointed corners at the top and bottom of the Mill Street side imply a flatiron brick building which might have had a separate existence, or is it the frontage of a more utilitarian part? The irony derives from using a warehouse idiom as a formal facade to another type of storage idiom. But the centre section of brickwork is cut back to respond to the geometry of the scalloped side, showing them to be as one.

To enjoy the fabulous view, the river facade is nearly all glass, making it immediately different from its small-apertured neighbours. The other necessary feature was bound to be the balconies to each living room. As visual support to all these balconies, the central rendered masonry form was created also which creates privacy. The client had already chosen the name of the development before the commission, so there must have been auto-suggestion operating in the pagoda-like appearance. The flanging of the openings, on the other hand, makes it read like a ship's steel construction. The colour is neither quite Chinese lacquer nor red oxide. The base columns join the main facade not with capitals but as bridge abutments to show their life of intermittent immersion. The plan geometry allows them to be splayed out to give a false perspective and is enhanced by a Magritte-like stern of a boat disappearing into the centre arch, which acts as a balcony to the ground floor. At mean average high tide, the keel of this boat will just touch the water. The drama of dockland has always been the juxtaposition of the conflicting scales of ships, cranes, buildings, and storage tanks. The building replaces the missing ships, but retains the natural floor-to-floor rhythm of a building.

Architecturally it can be read as a cross between the modernist expressionism of the Luban Chemical Factory by Poelzig and conversely as a florid Victorian hat stand. The vestigial nibs of brickwork at either side (a fire requirement) curve outward to allow the facade to project like a big bay window in the manner of the Art Nouveau Hotel at Ixelles by Rossenboom. The top part of the central feature is reined back by a slither of stone cornice, slightly crushing the glass on the fifth and sixth floors into a chamfer.

The building was referred by the ('no red tape') London Docklands Development Corporation to the Royal Fine Arts Commission who recommended it; seven months later it received planning permission.

ARCHITECTS Campbell, Zogolovitch, Wilkinson & Gough Architects
DESIGN TEAM Stephen Rigg & The Partners
STRUCTURAL ENGINEERS Alan Baxter & Associates
QUANTITY SURVEYORS E C Harris & Partners
DEVELOPMEMT COMPANY Jacob Island Co Ltd
MODEL Dominic Sagar

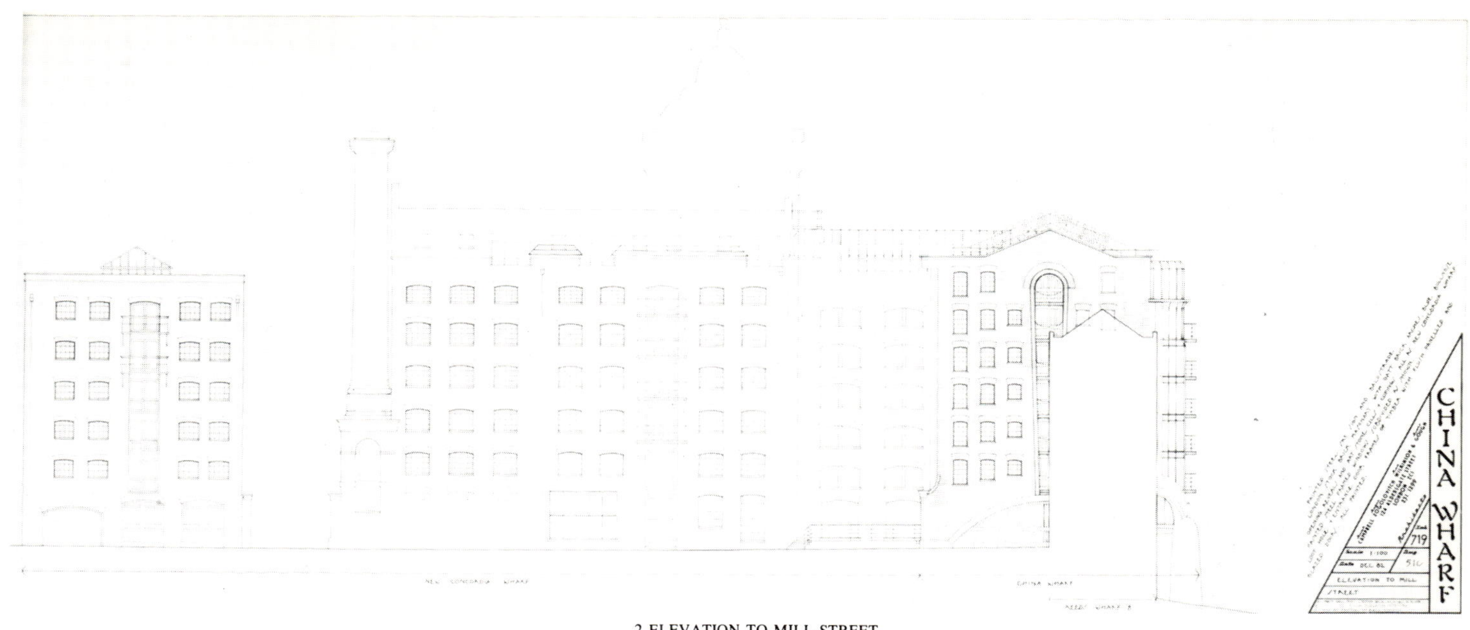

2 ELEVATION TO MILL STREET.

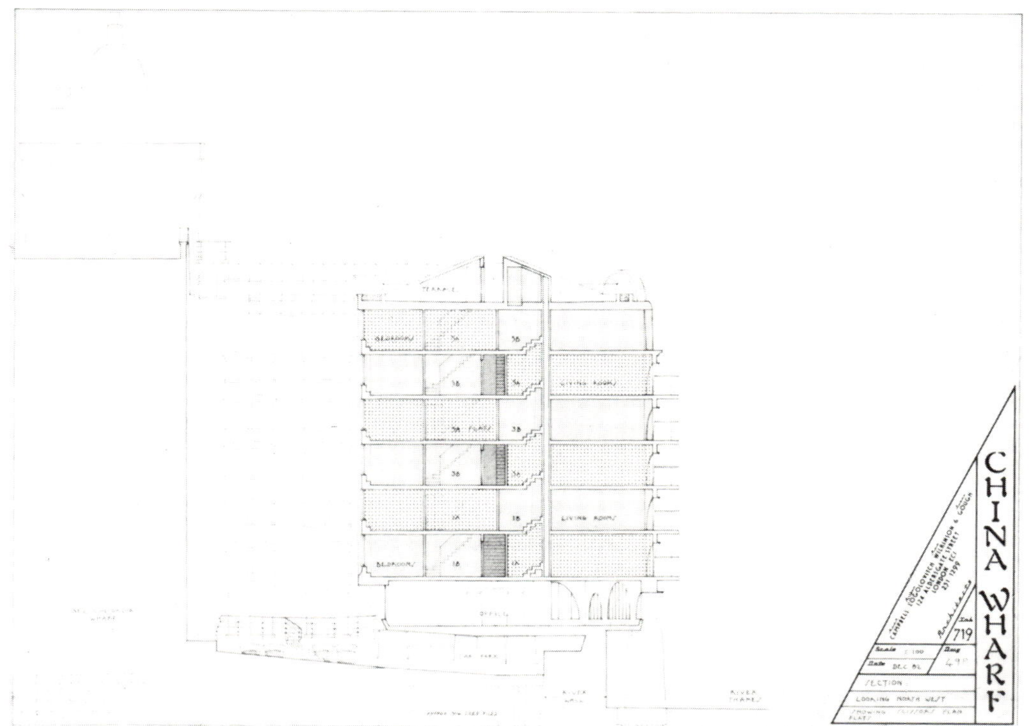

3 SECTION LOOKING NORTH-WEST.

4 GROUND FLOOR PLAN.

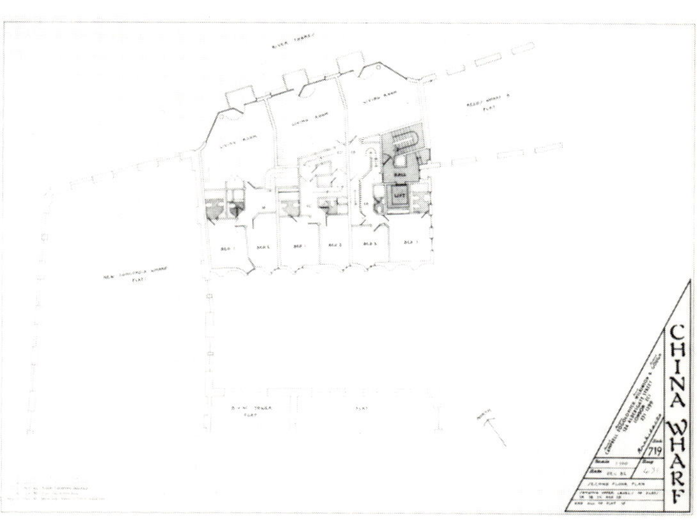

5 TYPICAL FLOOR PLAN.

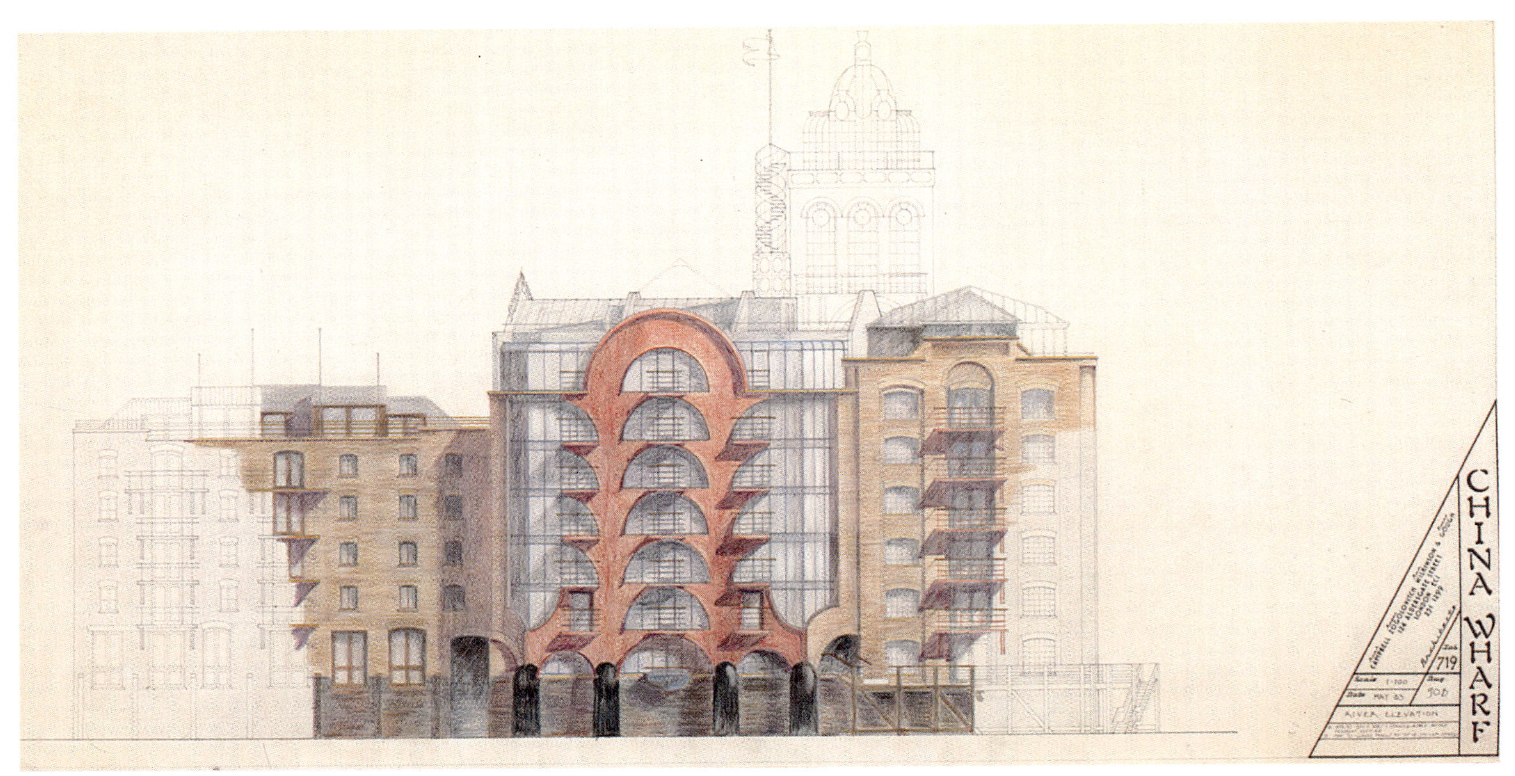

6 RIVER ELEVATION.

7 VIEW OF CHINA WHARF AND ITS NEIGHBOURS FROM MILL STREET.

Subscription Department,
ARCHITECTURAL DESIGN,
7/8 Holland Street,
London, W.8.

ARCHITECTURAL DESIGN SUBSCRIPTION

☐ I wish to subscribe to *AD* at the full rate.

☐ I wish to subscribe to *AD* at the student rate, and enclose proof of student status. (College .... Year ....)

☐ I claim a free subscription to *AD*, and enclose five new subscription orders (please attach names and addresses) and payments.

Starting date: Issue No .... Year ....

☐ Payment enclosed by: cheque/postal order/draft VALUE UK£/US$...........

☐ Please charge .... to my credit card.*

American Express - Diners Club - Access / Master Charge / Eurocard - Barclaycard / Visa

Account Number ....

Signature ....

Name ....

Address ....

....

....

* Credit cards will be charged in UK Sterling at current exchange rates.

Subscription Department,
ARCHITECTURAL DESIGN,
7/8 Holland Street,
London, W.8.

Architectural Design has for many years been internationally acknowledged as foremost among a small number of specialist publications devoted to providing up-to-date information on architecture of both the present and past. Each issue, fully illustrated with drawings and often specially commissioned colour and black and white photographs, contains a thematic Profile which constitutes a detailed study, contributed by leading critics, historians or practitioners, of a contemporary architect, trend, building type or historical theme of current relevance, together with a magazine section consisting of letters, book reviews, theoretical articles and news of recent buildings, projects and competitions. The high standard of writing, editorial selection and presentation within ***Architectural Design*** has made it one of the world's leading architectural magazines, and essential reading for discerning architects and students alike.

AD has a policy of active participation in architectural discourse, and as well as commissioning special Profiles with the aim of furthering architectural debate on topical issues such as the role of classicism within contemporary practice, the magazine also sponsors lectures, competitions such as the increasingly influential annual Project Awards and the recent popular Dolls' House competition, to promote and stimulate architectural thinking and practice. ***AD*** subscribers are entitled to participate in any of the events organized by the magazine.

SUBSCRIBE NOW and read the magazine that leads the rest!

SUBSCRIPTION RATES

Full annual subscription
UK & Eire £39.50 Overseas US$75.00(£49.50)

Special annual student rate
UK & Eire £35.00 Overseas US$65.00(£42.50)

NOTE: Subscriptions can be backdated.

AD* 'AGENTS'** collect five new subscriptions and we will give you a year's free subscription to ***AD. Please send your free subscription details together with details of the other five subscriptions with payment/credit card authority/ bank draft, direct to:-

Subscription Department,
ARCHITECTURAL DESIGN,
7/8 Holland Street,
London, W.8.

AD Profiles/back issues are available, please see overleaf for listing and order form.

ROGER HUNTLEY

Villas in the People's Park, Belsize Wood

1983 COMMENDATION

1 PERSPECTIVE OF VILLAS.

In contrast to the 'village in the city' mentality of recent decades, the project is offered as a 'memory of urbanism', making a clear separation between the buildings as a 'fragment of the city' and the gardens. Indeed, the engagement with nature is mediated through abstraction rather than nostalgia, which is perhaps nearer to the legacy of the Lawn Road Flats; this inspired the notion of the grid which represents the interface between the chaos of the site and the integration of the buildings; a mixed development of sixteen villas (64 units), a library and art centre, with tennis courts and a clubhouse in the park.

Two rows of villas address a central tree-lined reservation used for car parking, on the south-side the circular vent is 'absorbed' becoming the gateway to childrens' play areas. Public buildings act as bookends, marking the twin entrances to the park; at the north end the library tower signals the major vehicular entrance to the scheme which is confirmed by the gatehouse on Haverstock Hill. At the south end, the route from the underground station is pedestrianised as a walkway to the park. Here two elements define its major space, the promenade and the pergola: the first acts as a plinth to the villas while the second makes an edge to the tennis courts and leads to the clubhouse. This contains the changing facilities and the New Isobar as a tribute to the Isokon Furniture Company; it floats over the cutting on stilts. Off the pergola a walled garden offers a quiet refuge and mediates the formality of the courts.

The Villas

The illusory idea of a large house is achieved by the common entrances and double frontage; this is emphasised by the scale and modelling of the facades which recall the Georgian idea of classical fronts with functional backs, the stucco being returned to the flank walls and stopped short. Lower units are reached from the central formal doorways while upper units are off the common shared stairway in the 'gap' defined by the tall columns which also express the collective identity of the house at the scale of the street. Plans are relatively simple: three types have emerged through the concerns of orientation giving a north-east house and across the street a south-west house.

Although areas are small, circulation has been reduced to a minimum. The typologically 'sensible' plans would allow easy adaptation to either a four-storey 'big' house or three levels over a self-contained flat. Private open space is consciously minimal to emphasise the communal and public nature of the scheme. Construction would be of high density fairface blockwork with stuccoed facades and precise aluminium windows of the finest sections. Structurally the facades are treated as independant assemblages applied to the cross-wall construction of the building.

The Art Centre and Library

The weakness of programme invited the invention of relatively notional blocks which could be open to a variety of uses. The Art Centre consists of a central spine 'gallery' which links the two entrances to form a processional route through the building; the four-storey street element contains general activities, a cafe overlooking the park, and double height studios. At the rear, the exhibition space and workshops take up the 'wedge' of the site. A saw-tooth roof is controlled externally to reduce heat gain and internally for natural lighting levels. The building would function primarily as a workshop with occasional exhibitions, thus a high degree of expensive technology is not required. The library is entered via an open court at the base of the tower: this becomes the focus of the street and houses reading rooms and reception areas. At street level, shops animate the facades; these would be associated with the library so as not to compete with trade on Haverstock Hill. Internally the spaces are organised around a double height space glazed with a massive roof light, thus giving the building spatial unity. It is intended that maximum opportunity be given to future changes, hence the simplicity of the planning and pragmatic structure.

ARCHITECT Roger Huntley

WILL ALSOP, MIKE GOLD & JOHN LYALL
Tete Defense Competition, Paris, 1984

The major problem in preparing this scheme for the 1983 Tete Defense Competition in Paris was finding an appropriate method of closing the end of the city's great historic axis. The brief called for a communications/media version of the Pompidou Centre, a place where people might go to see exhibitions and to learn about media technologies; it also called for new offices for the Department of the Interior. Our proposal consists of a giant electronic screen (100metres × 100metres) that could be programmed to reflect the events contained in the communications centre, or the rest of the city. As an object, it represents a glittering, two-dimensional facade, in the best English tradition, as exemplified by the west front of Lincoln Cathedral. The aesthetic nature of the screen gave the clue to the architecture of the remainder of the buildings as being splendid, sparkling Teutonic solids, quietly hiding behind the screen.

ARCHITECTS Will Alsop, Mike Gold, John Lyall
STRUCTURAL ENGINEER Frank Newby of Felix J Samuely Partners

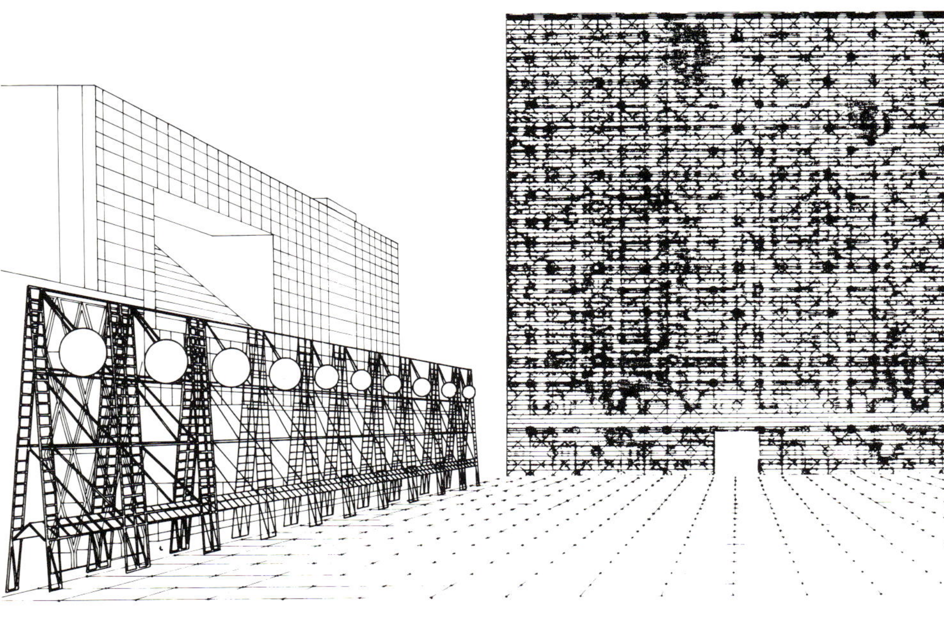

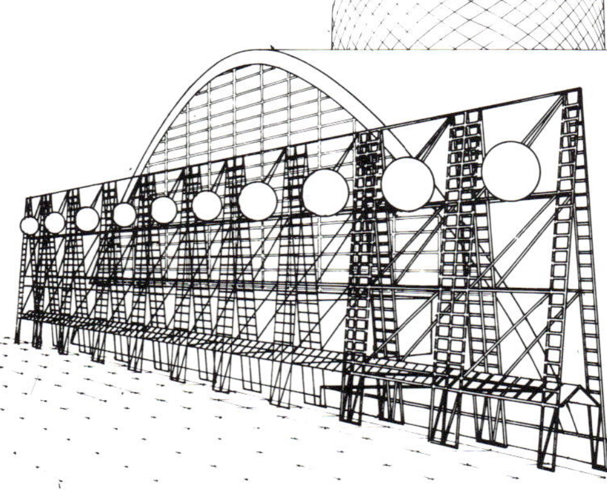

1 PERSPECTIVE VIEW OF ELECTRONIC SCREEN FROM SQUARE.

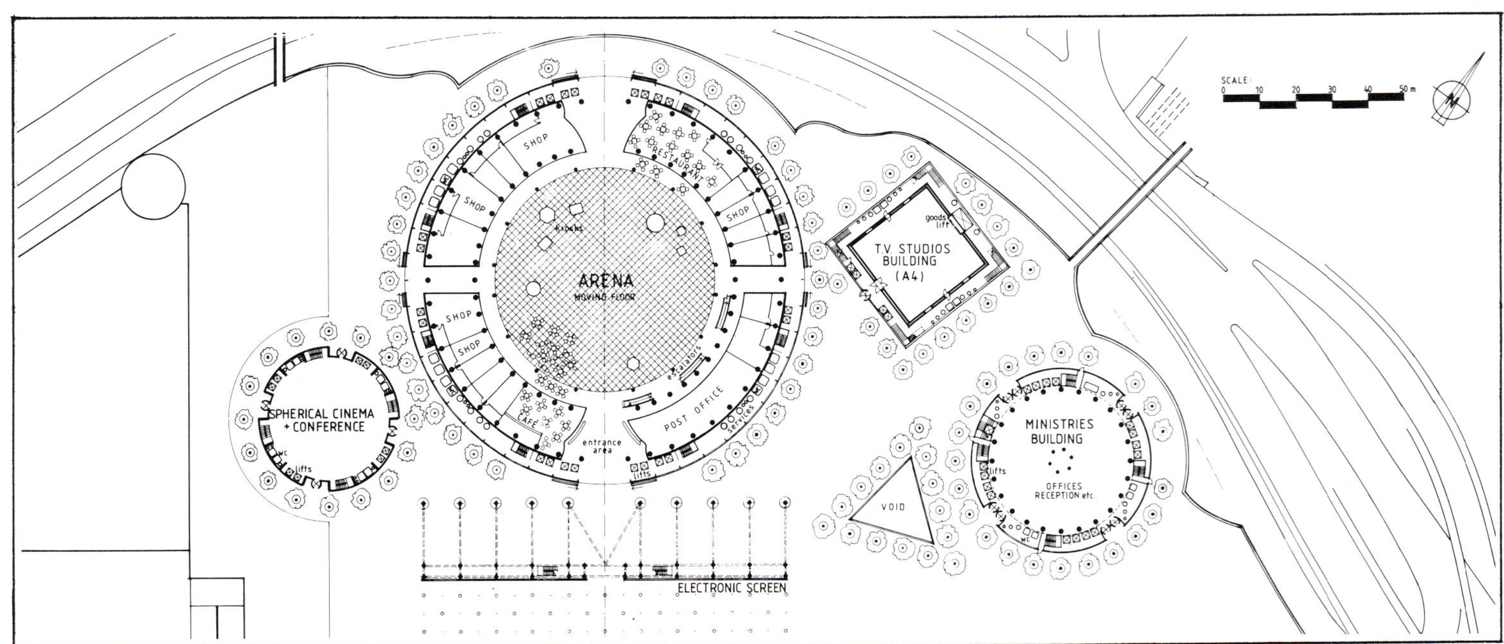

2 PLAN.

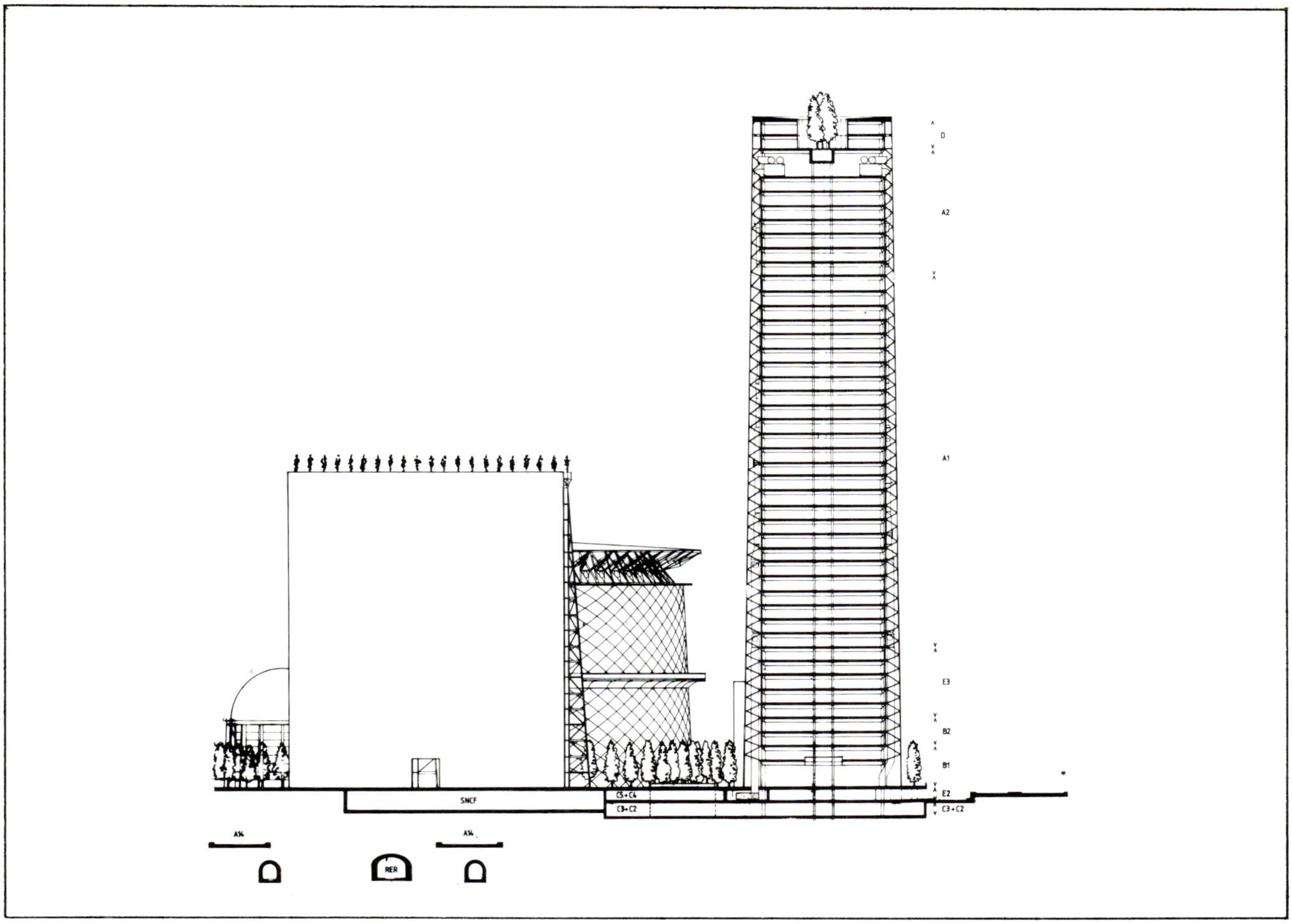

3 NORTH-SOUTH SECTION.

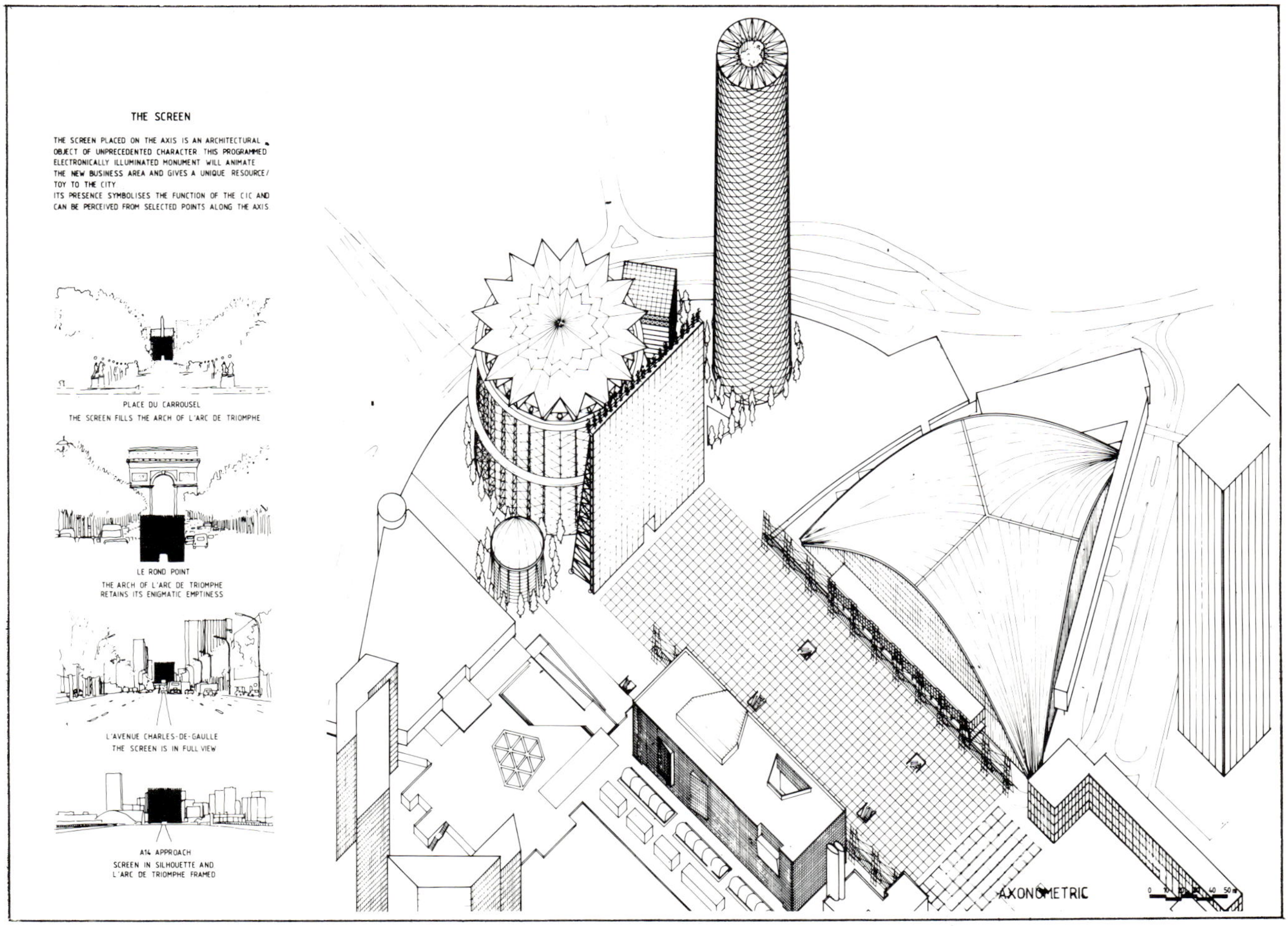

4 AXONOMETRIC AND AXIAL STUDIES OF SCREEN.

BRUCE GILBRETH ARCHITECTS
Trim Trail, Aztec West, Bristol 1984

1984 COMMENDATION

1 AERIAL VIEW OF SITE.

Brief
To design and construct a 'Trim Trail' along the Mall at Aztec West. The Trim Trail is a set of exercise stations forming part of a jogging route serving an estimated employee population of 7,500. 10,000 people.

Research
The Sports Council's handbook 'Trim Trails' established the series of exercises and types of stations required.

Material
Our research proved that the common use of timber (as in the Sports Council's handbook) had a tendency to split, rendering it dangerous and unsightly.

Form
When logs are used, the Trim Trail has a character more like a military training camp than Aztec West. This realisation led to considering other material, such as metal and plastic, which would allow for a 'richer' design, enabling the exercise machines to exist in their own right when not in use (i.e. garden sculptures).

Design Proposal
The setting is near both large, metal-clad, grid-ordered buildings and a rich and varied population of trees, shrubs and hedges. The machines, within the tradition of garden architecture (pavilions, follies, etc) were viewed as mediators between the two: an architectural landscape of formal nature and informal structure. Both the shapes and the colours are primary. Together with the large, exaggerated scale, they are to establish an architectural playground—a nursery in the landscape for people increasingly growing younger.

Programme
Under construction, to be completed in 1984.

ARCHITECTS Bruce Gilbreth Architects
PROJECT ARCHITECT Iannis Zachariades
CLIENT Electricity Supply Nominees Ltd
DEVELOPMENT MANAGEMENT Richard Ellis
STEEL FABRICATOR LWC Metal Fabrication Ltd
GENERAL CONTRACTOR E J Sheldrake

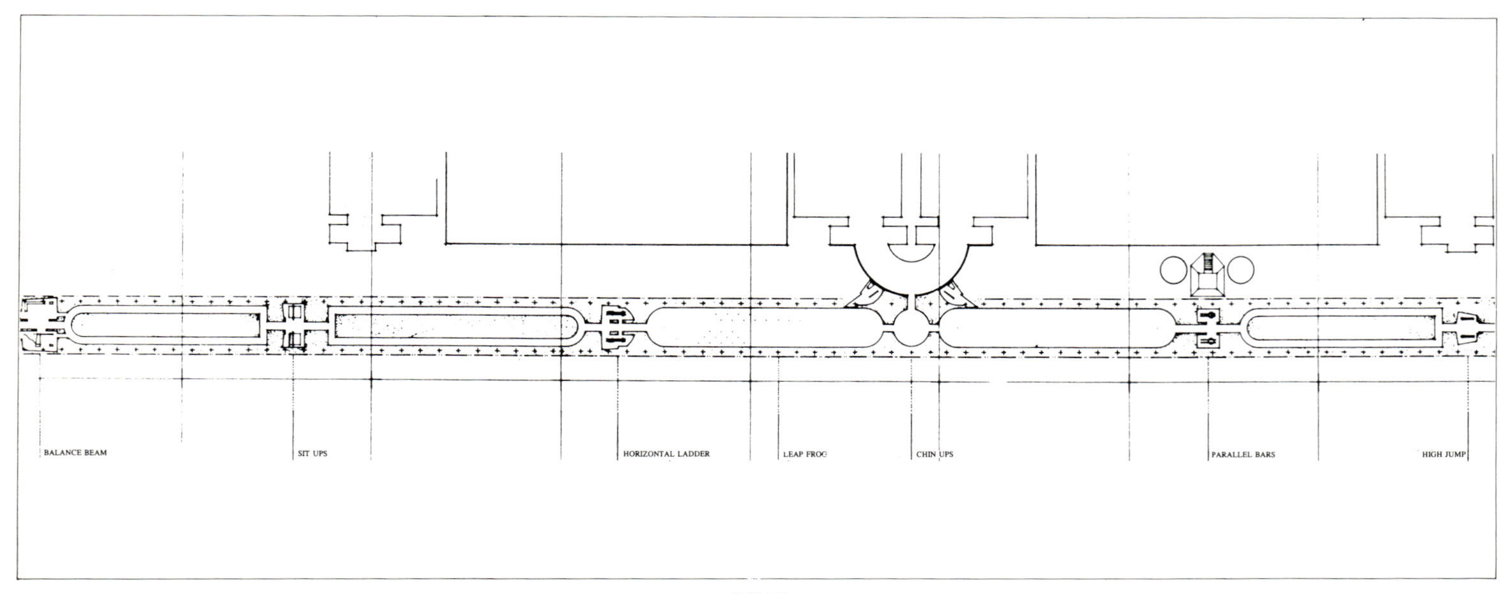

2 PLAN.

3 HIGH JUMP.

4 PARALLEL BARS.

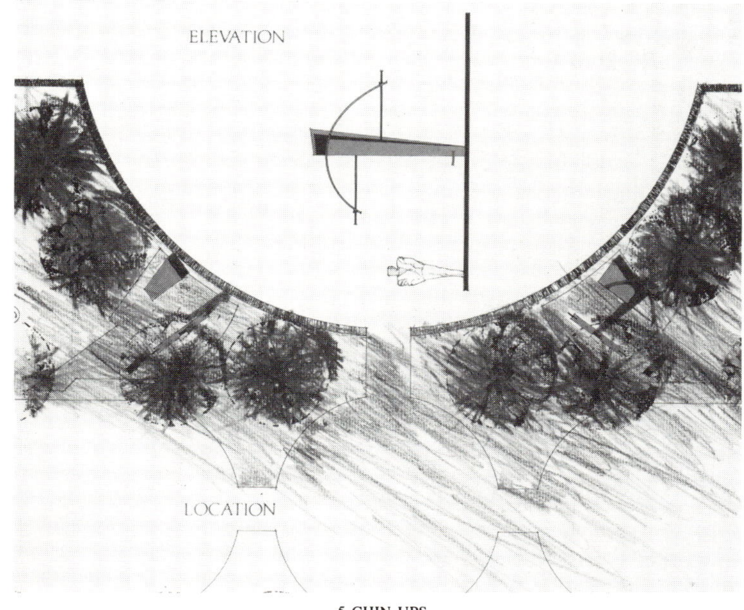

5 CHIN UPS.

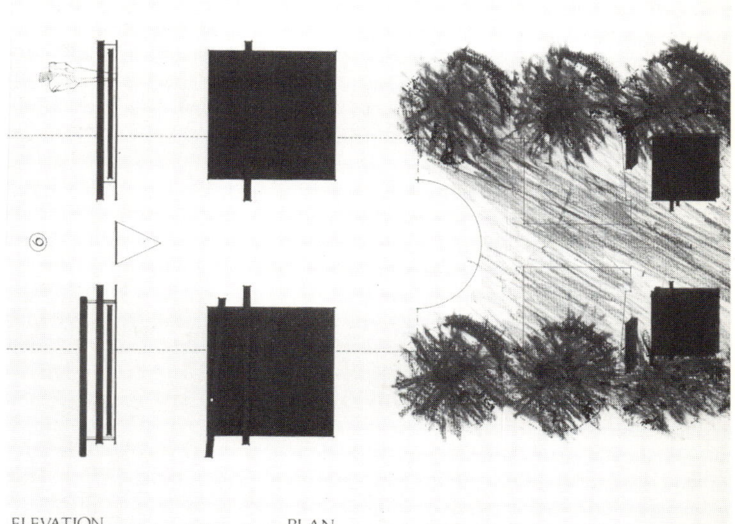

6 SIT UPS.

7 HORIZONTAL LADDER.

8 BALANCE BEAM. (PHS AUSTIN BROWN)

JOHN MUTLOW
(MUTLOW/DIMSTER ARCHITECTS)
Low Cost Housing Projects, Los Angeles, 1979–82

1983 AWARD

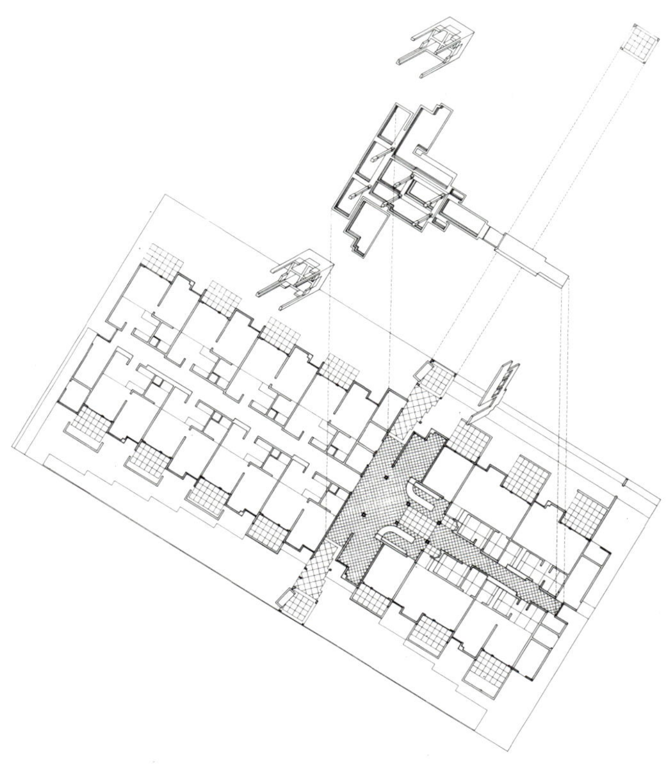

1 PLYMOUTH PLACE

Orientation around courtyards is the design formula for three low-cost housing projects, a spatial typology derived from the Mediterranean and well-adapted both for economic and climatic reasons to the California climate.

Two projects are for the elderly: Pico Villa (comprising 115 units in a predominantly Mexican inner city area) and Plymouth Place (64 units). The former, dubbed a 'Spanish Medieval Castle', is based on a system of components, the facades of which are painted a different pastel colour to heighten the Mediterranean effect. The latter project is based on a series of circulation spaces: entry through a gazebo culminates in a major interior gathering space. In their detailing and decoration these dwelling units pay homage to the minimalist typology of the Bauhaus rather than Post-Modern eclecticism.

The third project is the Cabrillo Village Farmworkers' Co-operative Housing, quadruplexes comprising 35 units organised as courtyard houses surrounding private back gardens. A major feature of the design is the passive solar space-heating system.

Diamond Beach Residence takes into account the client's desire for privacy and maximum relationship with the beach, and raising the main level of the house achieves both these ends.

PROJECT Pico Union Villa
ARCHITECT John V Mutlow
CLIENT Pico Union Neighbourhood Council
STRUCTURAL ENGINEER Dimitri K Vergun
ENERGY John V Mutlow
LANDSCAPE ARCHITECTS Barrio Planners Inc
GENERAL CONTRACTOR Campbell Construction Company
COST $3,000,000
PHOTOGRAPHY John V Mutlow, Sarah Dennison

PROJECT Plymouth Place
ARCHITECTS John V Mutlow/Mutlow Dimster Partnership
CLIENT Retirement Housing Foundation
STRUCTURAL ENGINEER Ronald Rogahn
ENERGY John V Mutlow
LANDSCAPE ARCHITECTS Barrio Planners Inc
GENERAL CONTRACTOR Shepherd and Green
COST $3,000,000
PHOTOGRAPHY John V Mutlow

PROJECT Cabrillo Village Farmworkers' Co-operative Housing
ARCHITECTS John V Mutlow/Mutlow Dimster Partnership
CLIENT Cabrillo Village Farmworkers' Co-operative
STRUCTURAL ENGINEER Hitoshi Tatsugawa
ENERGY John V Mutlow
LANDSCAPE ARCHITECTS Barrio Planners Inc
GENERAL CONTRACTOR McGall Contractors
COST $1,450,000
PHOTOGRAPHY Tim Street-Porter

PROJECT Diamond Beach Residence
ARCHITECTS John V Mutlow/Mutlow Dimster Partnership
CLIENT Mr and Mrs Robert Diamond
STRUCTURAL ENGINEER Dimitri K Vergun
ENERGY John V Mutlow
LANDSCAPE ARCHITECTS Barrio Planners Inc
GENERAL CONTRACTOR John Giff
COST $175,000
MODEL James Hansen
PHOTOGRAPHY John V Mutlow, Sarah Dennison

2 PICO UNION VILLA.

3 DIAMOND BEACH RESIDENCE.

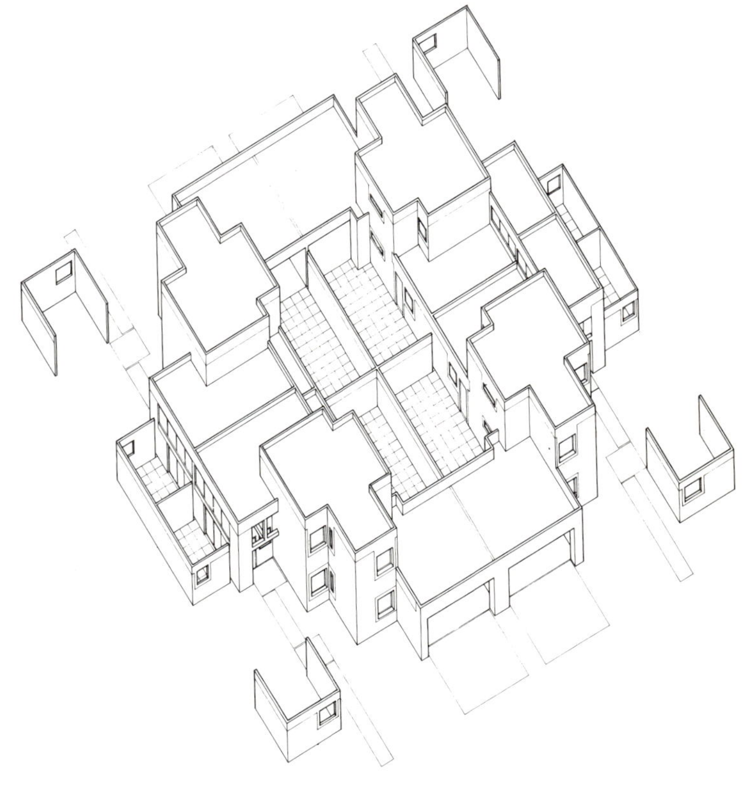

4 CABRILLO VILLAGE.

1 CUT-AWAY AERIAL PERSPECTIVE: PROPOSED ERECHTHEION LEFT, PAVED AREA CENTRE, ROYAL SCOTTISH ACADEMY RIGHT, NATIONAL GALLERY TOP.

ALLIES & MORRISON
The Mound, Edinburgh, 1983

1984 AWARD

2 PERSPECTIVE FROM PRINCES STREET.

A Major Public Space For Edinburgh
The primary design objectives of this submission, the division of the site into two distinct spaces, the concentration of pedestrian routes through the space and the manipulation of levels to dramatise the approaches to the two buildings are apparent in the drawings. There are, however, four specific proposals which require detailed explanation: all of these proposals would contribute to the success of the scheme, but they are not necessarily interdependent.

In order to intensify public use of the site, our design makes provision for the construction of a row of small pavilions like Roman shops, to be let on short or shared leases (allowing use, as at Covent Garden in London, one day a week by craftsmen); from these, goods could be sold in winter, refreshments sold in summer and information distributed during the festival. At first, only one might be built in permanent materials and the rest could be assembled as temporary structures—if they prove successful (socially and commercially), they could in time all be constituted in stone, and in this form provide maximum protection to the new square from the easterly wind.

In one building (Erechtheion) at the Princes Street end of the site are combined an information centre (in the loggia) and the relocated telephone kiosks—waiting to use the phone may become a pleasure. The rear wall of the information office is glazed, opening up a rarely experienced vista down the length of Princes Street Gardens between the two rows of trees.

As it stands, the entrance to the Royal Scottish Academy can no longer be regarded as successful—one cannot enter the building on its axis (too much traffic) and it faces north. What is still remarkable, however, is the axial view of the entrance facade from George Street and the axial view from the top of the steps across to the hills of Fife. We propose some modifications to encourage the passer-by to mount the steps and have provided more space (and railings to lean on at the top). Ideally we would suggest re-siting the public entrance to the south facade and using the northern section of the building as a coffee shop enjoying the view and the activity on Princes Street.

One real inducement for the public to use the new space would be a major link with the north side of Princes Street, providing a route for everybody from the shops to the galleries, the gardens, the castle and the High Street. We therefore propose extending elements of the paving across the roadway to define a wide pedestrian crossing, and moving the traffic lights further east accordingly.

Materials have been chosen to define further the two spaces: stone paving for the square and granite setts for the upper terrace. The permanent buildings would be constructed of stone with lead-faced roofs. The intention is that the detailing would be both elegant and simple, as befits the city.

The cost has been estimated at £420–440,000 assuming the construction of one permanent pavilion and the manufacture of eleven temporary pavilions. This figure would include all light fittings, benches and loose furniture for shared use by customers of the pavilions. The remainder of the budget would provide for the subsequent erection of a monument (to some as yet undefined person or event) on a site on the upper terrace, and also, if desired, for the construction of more permanent pavilions at the initial stage.

This scheme was awarded first prize in a competition to design a new public open space in the centre of Edinburgh. The project is scheduled to start on site at the end of this year.

ARCHITECTS Allies and Morrison
CLIENT Lothian Regional Council and Property Services Agency (Scotland)

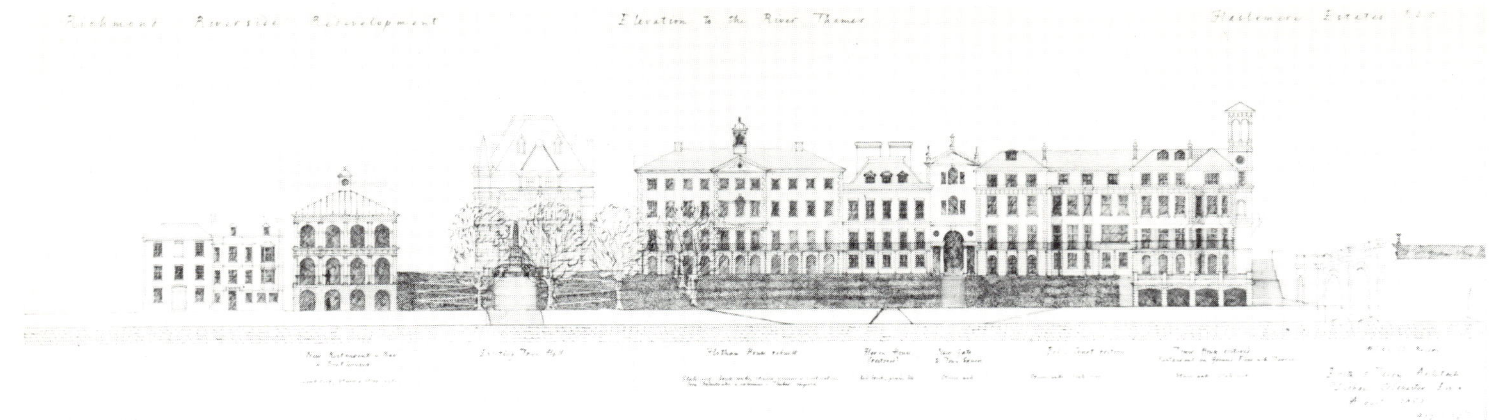

1 ELEVATION TO THE RIVER THAMES.

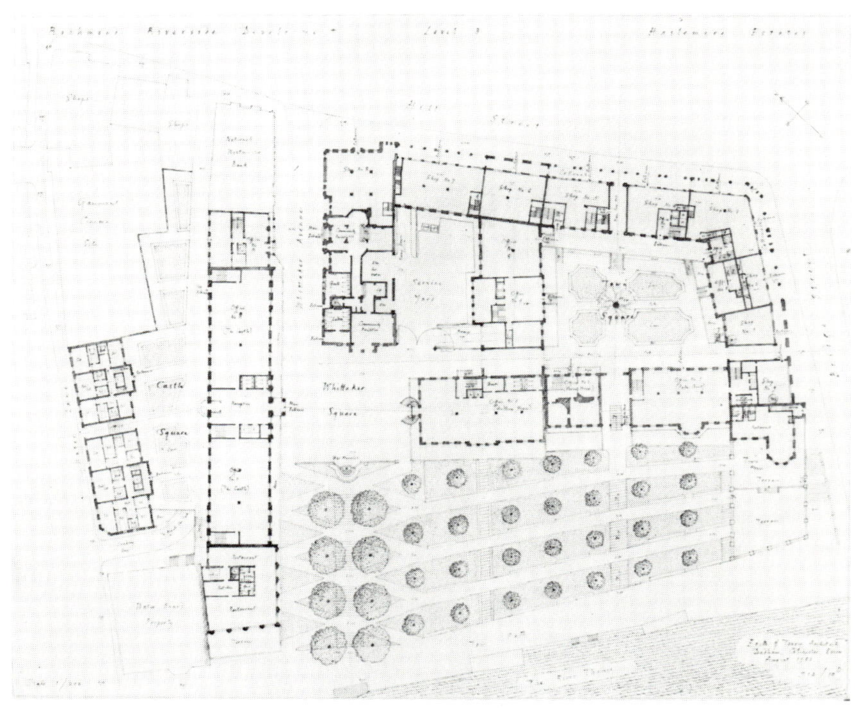

2 PLAN, LEVEL 3.

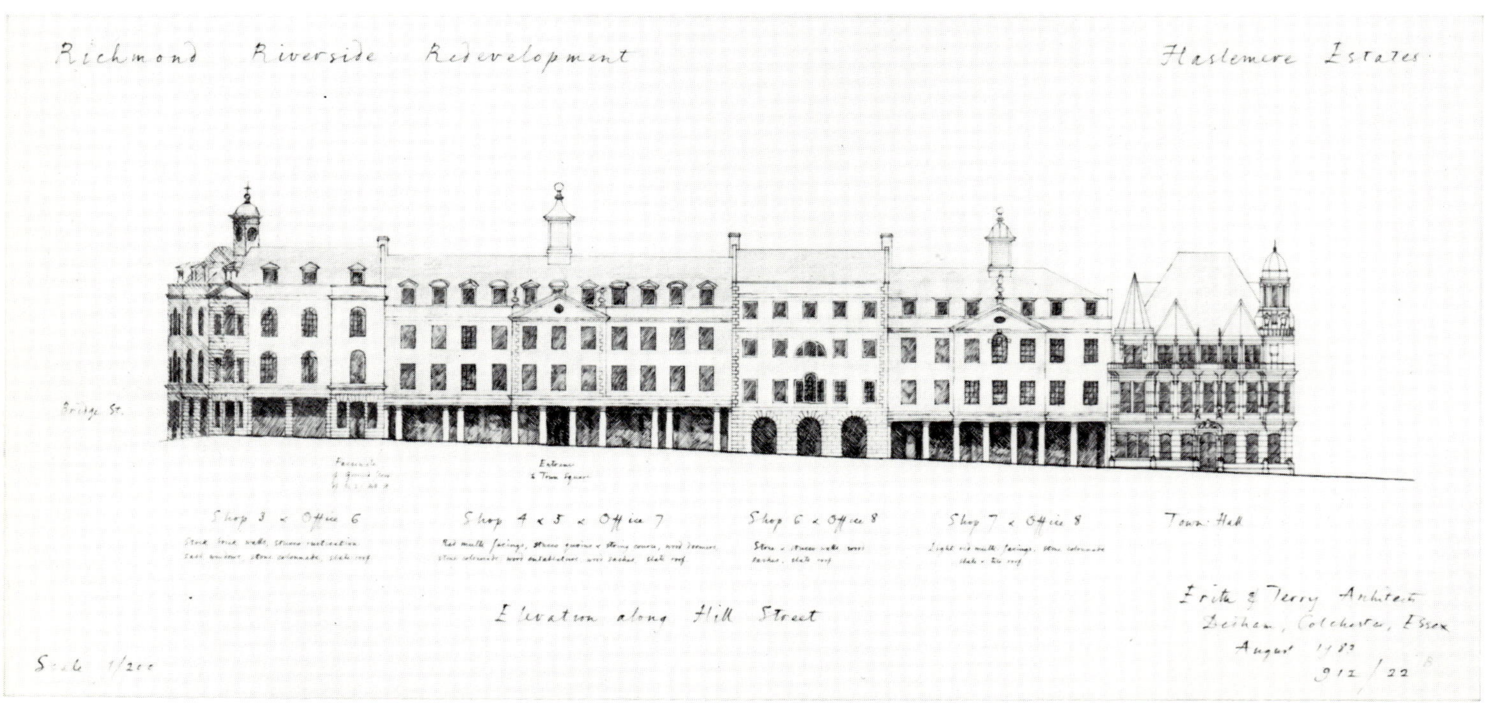

3 ELEVATION ALONG HILL STREET.

ERITH & TERRY
Richmond Riverside Development, 1983
1984 AWARD

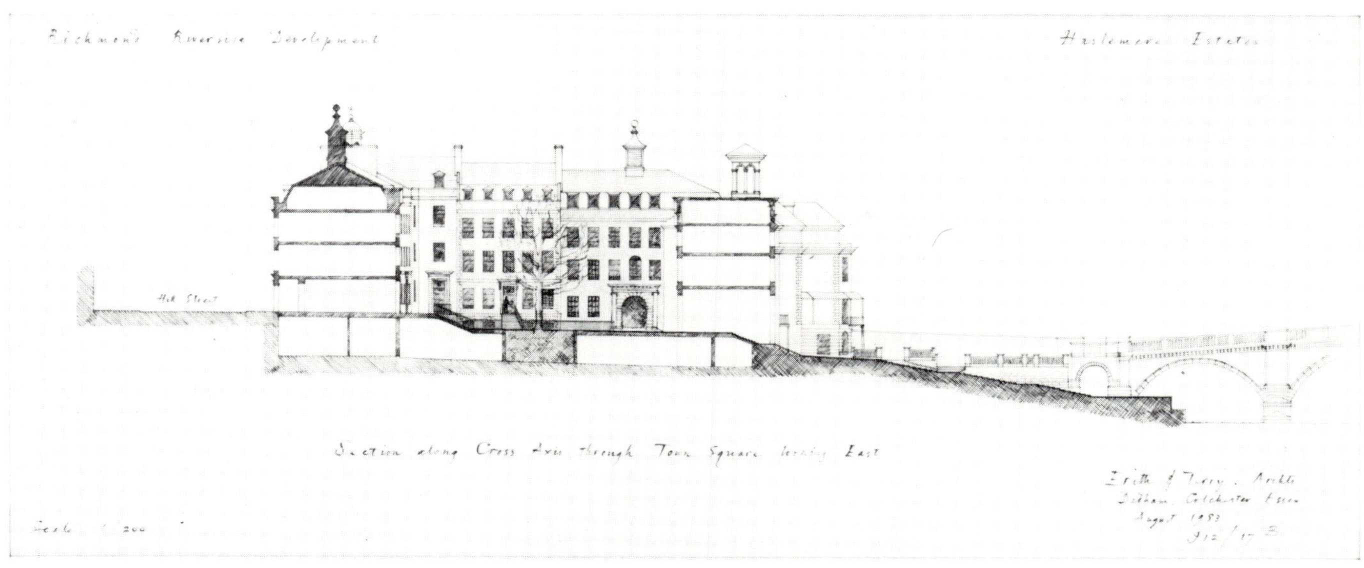

4 SECTION ALONG CROSS AXIS THROUGH TOWN SQUARE LOOKING EAST.

The whole development can be divided into three architectural components: the street, the river front and the square.

The Street

The facades along Bridge and Hill Street consist of small individual buildings over a colonnade. This type of development not only maintains the scale and character of Richmond as it was in the eighteenth century, but is the most natural way of accommodating the slope of the site. Thus, separate buildings have different levels inside the roof line and foundation expressing their hillside position. The pavement runs inside the stone colonnade which extends the whole length of the elevation with columns or arches related to the size of the buildings above them. The street front is set back from Tower House allowing full view of the Tower. The buildings are constructed in loadbearing brickwork with stucco and stone dressings, timber and windows, some with boxes on the face and others in the late Georgian manner with the sashes set in reveals with thin glazing bars. The walls finish with parapets with pitched and mansard roofs in slate and tile and dormer windows.

Each building is treated separately; for instance, shop No 3 on the corner of the Bridge Street and Hill Street merits a more imposing elevation based on the rusticated front of Jarvis' (29 Hill Street).

All shops are accessible within the colonnade and all have stairs to basement storage and lavatories. These storage areas are easily accessible from the goods lift in the service yard.

The River Front

The river front is the 'garden elevation' of the site. Classical facades in brick and stucco with sash windows, slate roofs and dormers are seen above the trees from the river and Richmond Bridge.

Whenever possible, the original buildings along the river will be restored and the facade unchanged. In detail the riverside front would be made up as follows:

a) Tower House was designed by Laxton in 1856. The elevations to the river and Bridge Street would remain but the internal layout would be altered to incorporate a restaurant on level 2 with access to the existing terraces on top of the boat house. The upper floors will be converted to form 2 flats per floor.

b) Palm Court was built in the 1850s and suffered many alterations when it was joined with Heron House and used as a hotel. The elevation facing the Thames would remain, the inside would be rebuilt and the elevation facing Town Square would also be rebuilt on the lines of the existing design. It will be faced in stucco with slate roof.

c) The gate between Palm Court and Heron House: this would replace the 1930s building linking Palm Court with Heron House and would now form the focal point from the river up through Town Square to Hill Street. It would be constructed in brickwork faced in stucco with stone dressings.

d) Heron House: this listed building was built in 1716 and will be completely repaired.

e) Hotham House will be a new building in brick with stucco quoins and rustications, stone steps and iron balconies and railings. Beyond Hotham House the view opens out into Whittaker Square, where the War Memorial now stands, to be the central point at the top of a wide and gently ascending axis of stone steps from the river.

The gardens are laid out in the classical manner with stone steps, intersecting ramps and terraced walks between formally planted trees. The levels in the garden terraces are worked out to coincide with the terraces of the Tower House restaurant. The use of intersecting ramps not only provides the characteristic classic architectural layout so successfully used in the great gardens at Tivoli, Villa Lante and the Villa Borghese but also allows complete freedom for prams and wheelchair users.

The Square

Behind the street and the river front facades lies the heart of the development: the square. Like an Oxford or Cambridge College or a classical villa, this scheme has its public front, its garden facade and its inner court—peaceful, enclosed and complete. Town Square is to be one of those spaces where simple architecture surrounds a pleasant garden; quiet for work inside or recreation outside. It should have the quality of the Inns of Court or a college or a small London Square. Four archways in stone and stucco lead through the buildings to Hill Street and the River on the cross axis, and the Bridge Street and Whittaker Square on the main axis.

A similar approach has been adopted for Castle Square which is accessible from Hill Street, Whittaker Square and Water Lane.

These squares are traffic-free and all the offices are accessible from the basement car parks.

Whittaker Square has been reorganised to relate more obviously to the riverside walk and the new

5 PERSPECTIVE VIEW OF DEVELOPMENT

gardens. The levels have been realigned and a very gentle slope below the war memorial will form a natural amphitheatre for Armistice Day ceremonies or other gatherings.

The existing Town Hall built in 1893 by W.G. Ancell has been planned for community use with minor external alterations and a restored roof. Although not a listed building, it is too good to pull down and one particularly likes the entrance, grand staircase and the main Council Chamber overlooking Whittaker Square, all of which will be restored. Further up Whittaker Avenue another existing building will be refurbished to accommodate office No 10.

The Castle on the west side of the square was

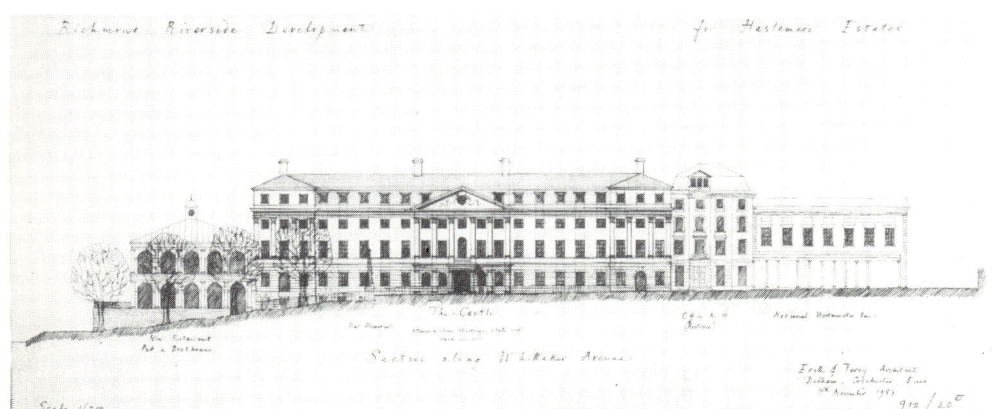

6 SECTION ALONG WHITTAKER AVENUE.

FROM RICHMOND BRIDGE.

designed in 1836. It has sentimental value but is unscholarly in its detail, having an asymmetrical classical facade and a superimposed order with a central pilaster. It has not been listed for good reason. The new design has elements of the original in the central pediment, stucco facade and slate roof but it is inspired to a greater extent by Sir William Chambers' fourth design for Richmond Palace. It was felt that a long building on this important site calls for this type of English Palladian detail.

The Water Lane side of Castle Square is taken up with a small residential building of three storeys and attic. Again, a simple formal gardens would be laid out in this square.

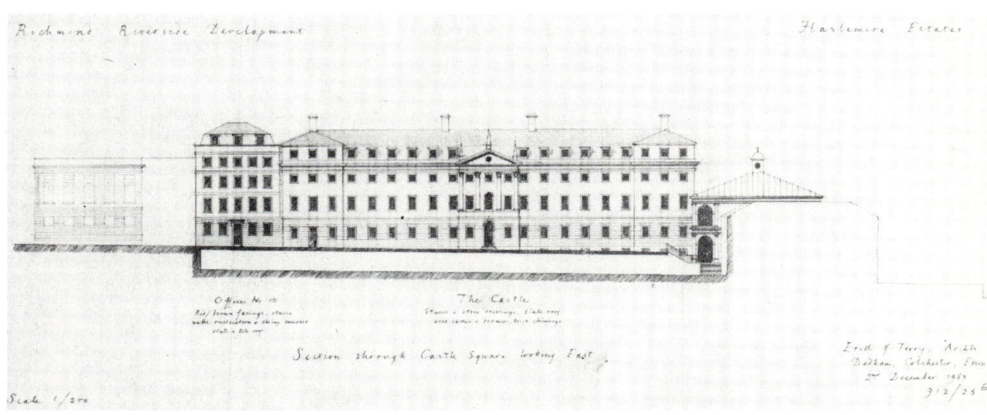

7 SECTION THROUGH CASTLE SQUARE LOOKING EAST.

MACCORMAC JAMIESON & PRICHARD ARCHITECTS
J Sainsbury Supermarket, Canterbury, Kent

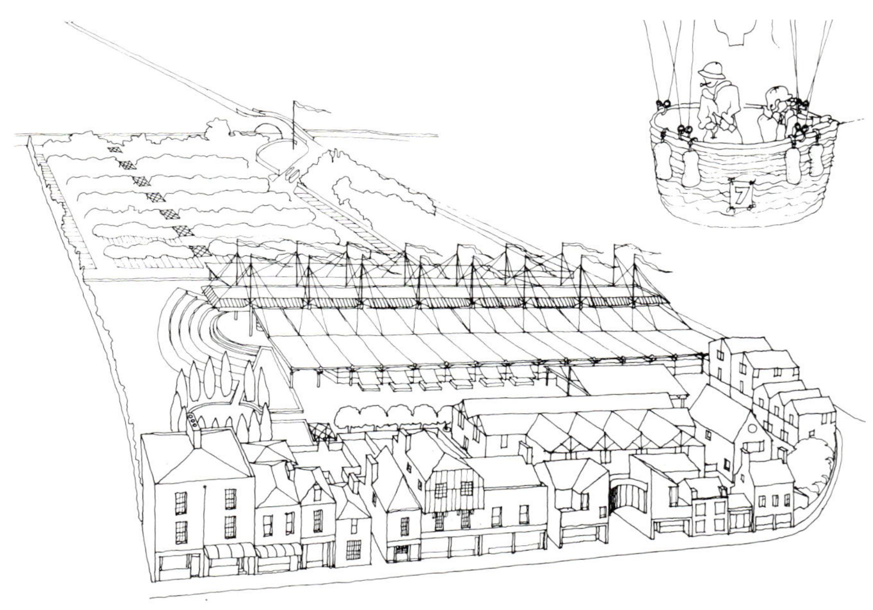

1 AERIAL PERSPECTIVE.

Supermarkets are difficult to relate to context. Although extensive in area they are low and virtually constant in internal section. They are basically warehouses which only offer a facade to the customer.

This project sets out to make a number of metaphorical allusions. The masts and rigging make a ship. Canterbury Cathedral is also like a great ship, stranded in the town. The suspended roof makes a marquee with associations of markets and festivities appropriate to a building sited adjacent to meadows used for sports and recreation.

The entrance facade is interpreted as a proscenium before which a landscaped amphitheatre is formed which can make use of the car park in evenings and at weekends. There are other associations suggested by the building's anatomy of spine and wings. Together these allusions transcend the more obvious Hi-Tech expression of the mast and tie structure.

The intention of the structural design is to reduce the weight of steel and therefore the cost while allowing rapid construction, using standard steel components. Piled concrete clad steel columns at 14 and 7 metre centres act as cantilevers from the ground. The central pairs of columns are spanned by 14 metre universal castellated beams clad in concrete, supporting a concrete floor to provide the upper floor with two hours fire resistance. Steel masts are sleeved and bolted to the tops of the beams to keep the tie-rods clear of the accommodation. They are attached to outriggers.

The shell over the staff accommodation is supported by steel portal frames which also support horizontal trussed cills which have the effect of increasing the top flange of the castellated beams where they are in mid-span compression.

The roof consists of 500mm deep universal beams at 7 metre centres suspended by the rods in mid-span. The horizontal component of compression is taken up by the concrete floor of the upper level construction. Purlins span at 3 metre centres and are decked with planger and rigid insulation.

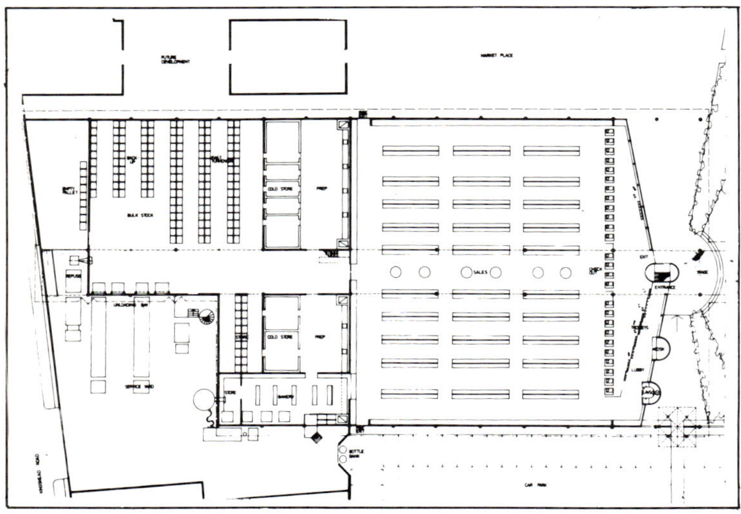

2 GROUND FLOOR PLAN.

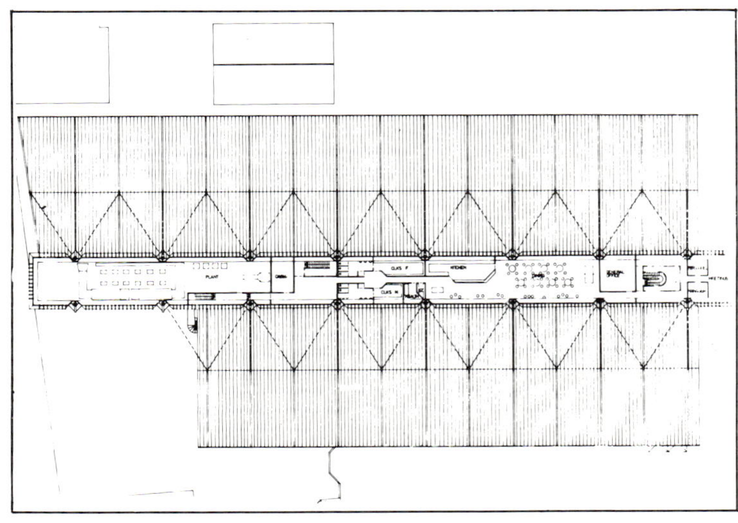

3 FIRST FLOOR PLAN.

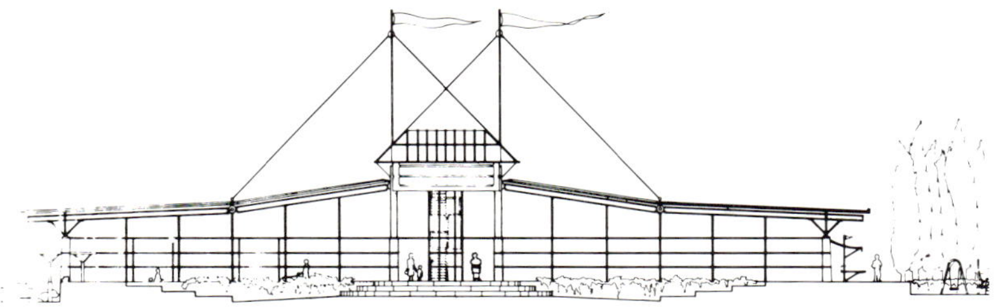

4 FRONT ELEVATION.

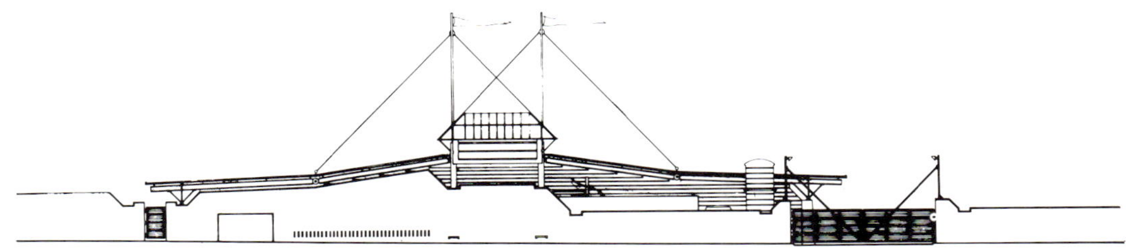

5 REAR ELEVATION.

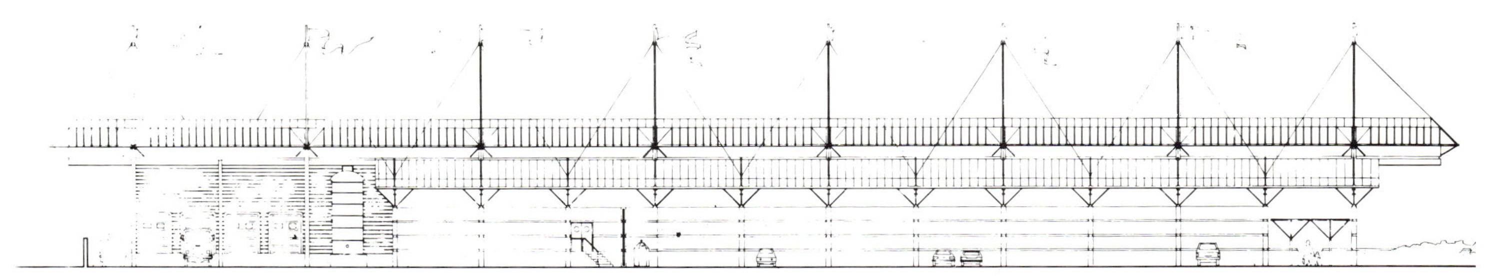

6 SIDE ELEVATION.

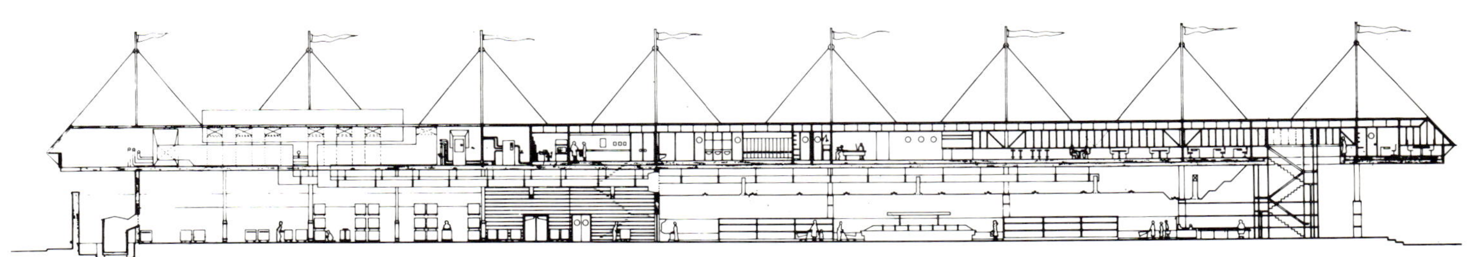

7 LONG SECTION.

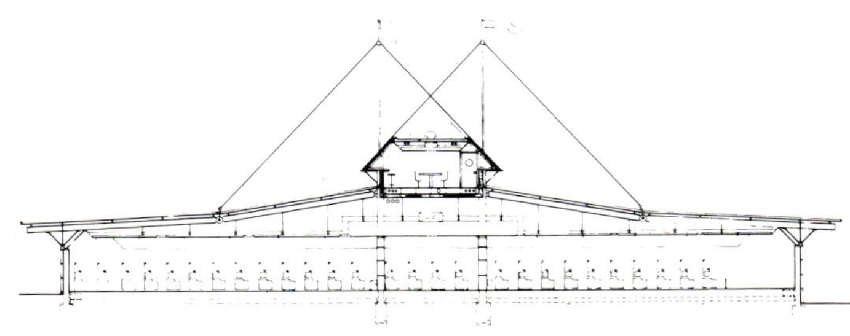

8 SECTION THROUGH SALES AREA.

RICK MATHER ARCHITECTS
New Climatic Research Building, University of East Anglia, Norwich 1983-5

1984 AWARD

The Climatic Research Unit will form part of the collection of new works which together help to organise the forgotten north side of the University campus.

Both as a gatehouse to the new Education, Computer Studies and Accountancy building, and as a round object in juxtaposition to the existing 'field' of the teaching 'wall', the CRU building will act as a focal point to define and reinforce the route from the University entrance down to the Sainsbury Centre at the opposite end of the 'wall'.

The curved white Spectra Glaze facade will be articulated with grey bands to imply a base and cornice, with vertical lines in between to scale up the wall from a storey height to the overall height of the building. This is in response to the similar organisation of the east facade of the EDU/CSA building, thus appropriating the landscape in between.

Spectra Glaze masonry is a lightweight expanded clay aggregate backing block, faced on one or more sides. Working in co-operation with the architects Spectra Glaze produced the special range of grey colours for use around the windows and as bands of colour against the predominantly off-white building. The masonry units, completely impervious to climatic effects, are available in 64 shades, for use internally or externally.

The cylindrical form of the CRU building will be cut and pushed in to signify the pedestrian route running through, to emphasise the smooth 'skin', and to expose the internal organisation of the building to the passer-by. Offices, library, common room and service rooms will be arranged around the central stair-hall in a rectangular plan. The stair-well will be covered with a roof-light to remind the researchers of the sky and weather instruments on the roof terrace.

The building was started on site in April of this year and is due to be completed in May 1985.

ARCHITECTS Rick Mather Architects
DESIGN TEAM Mark Guard, Bill Greensmith, Jim Conti, David Naessens
CLIENT University of East Anglia
STRUCTURAL ENGINEER Martin Hargreaves: Alan Baxter & Associates
SERVICES John Swaine & Mark Turner: Helix
QUANTITY SURVEYORS Mike Cable & David Francis: Stockings & Clarke

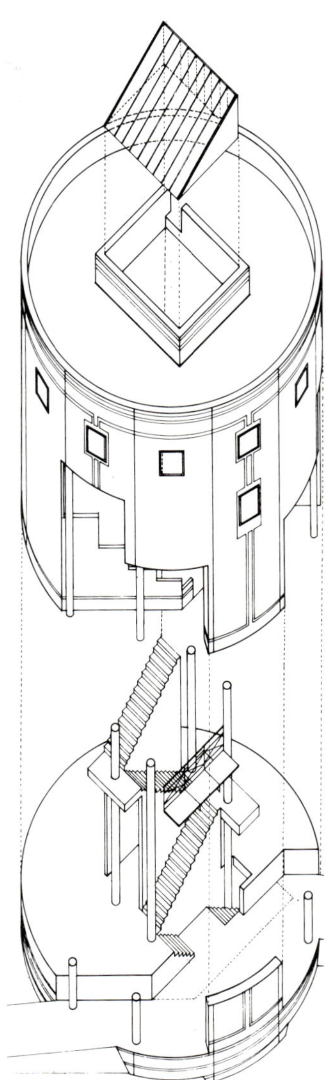

1 EXPLODED AXONOMETRIC.

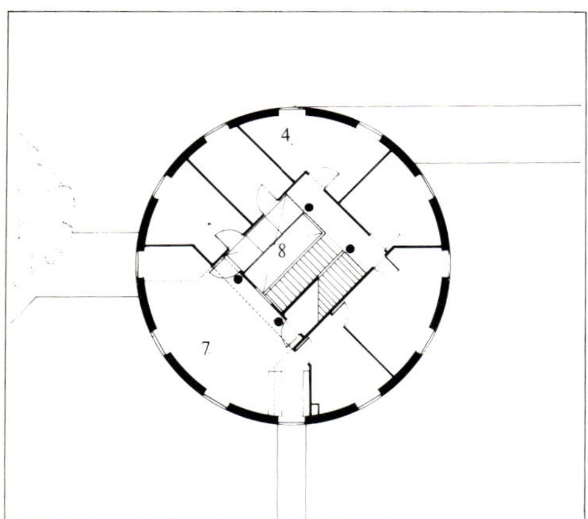

2 SECOND FLOOR PLAN.

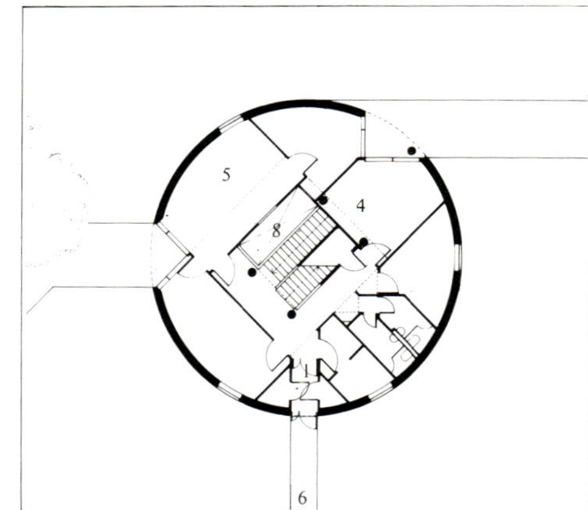

5 FIRST FLOOR PLAN.

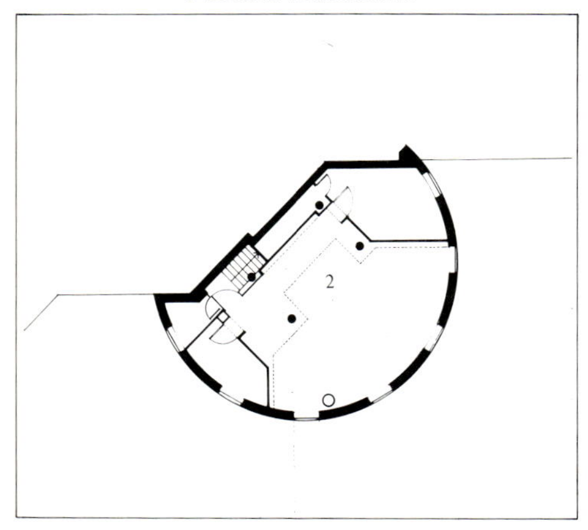

3 BASEMENT PLAN.

4 MODEL.

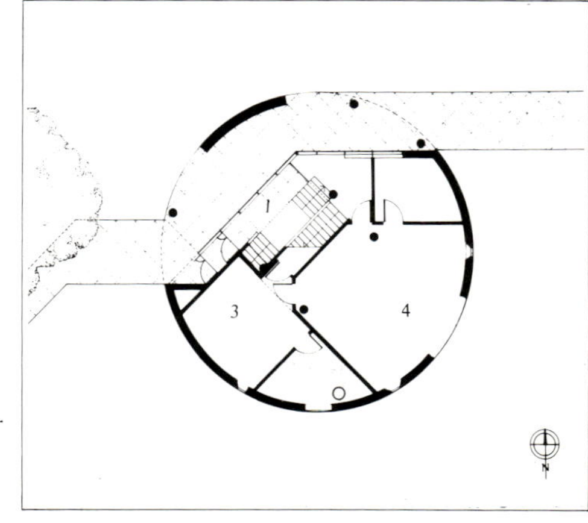

6 GROUND FLOOR PLAN.

7 SECTION/ELEVATION.

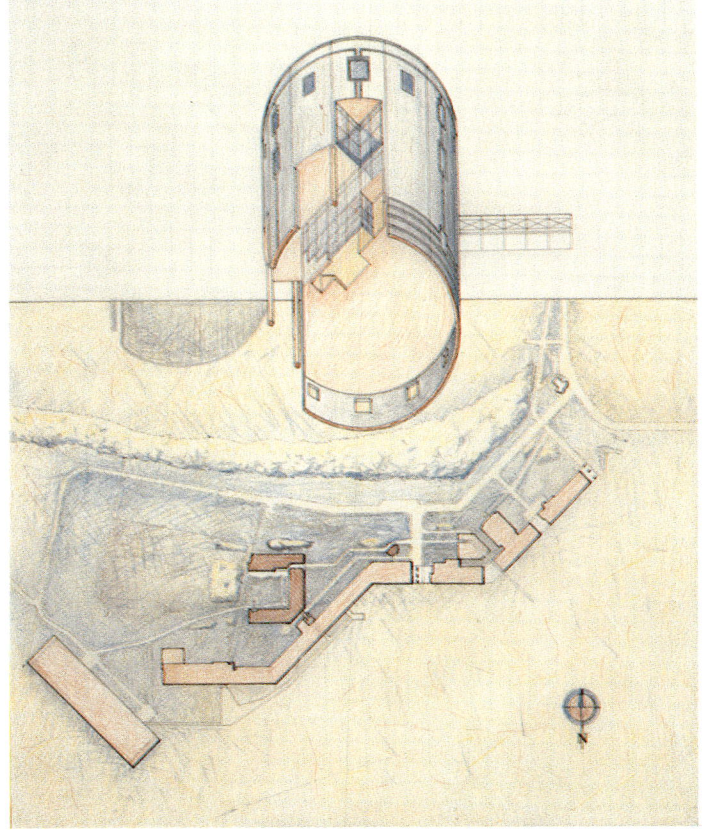

KEY
1 ENTRANCE
2 LIBRARY
3 COMPUTER
4 OFFICES
5 GENERAL OFFICE
6 LINK TO TEACHING HALL
7 COMMON ROOM
8 VOID

8 UP-AXONOMETRIC AND SITE PLAN.

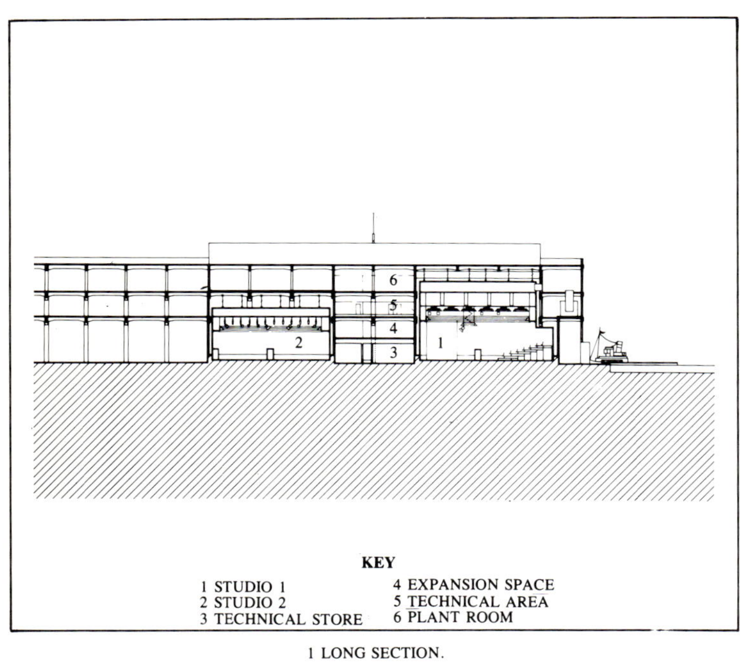

1 LONG SECTION.

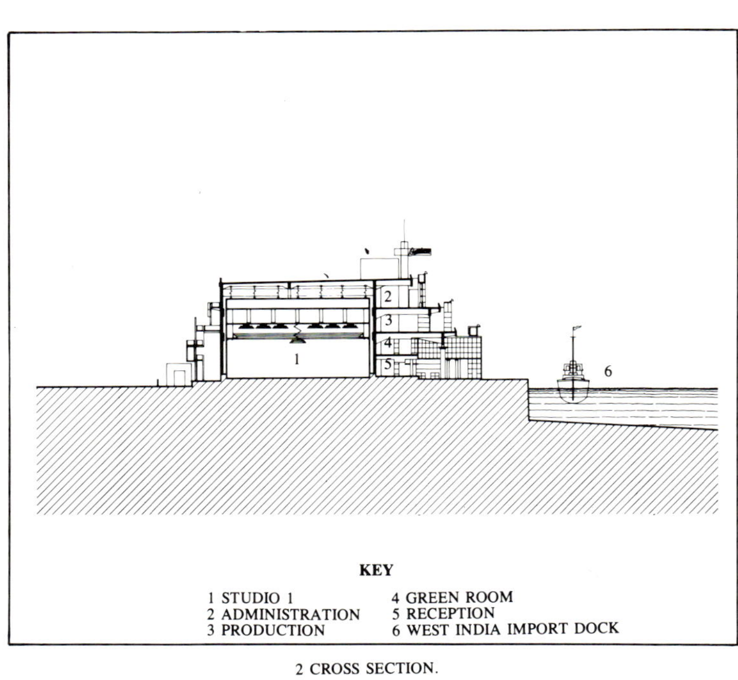

2 CROSS SECTION.

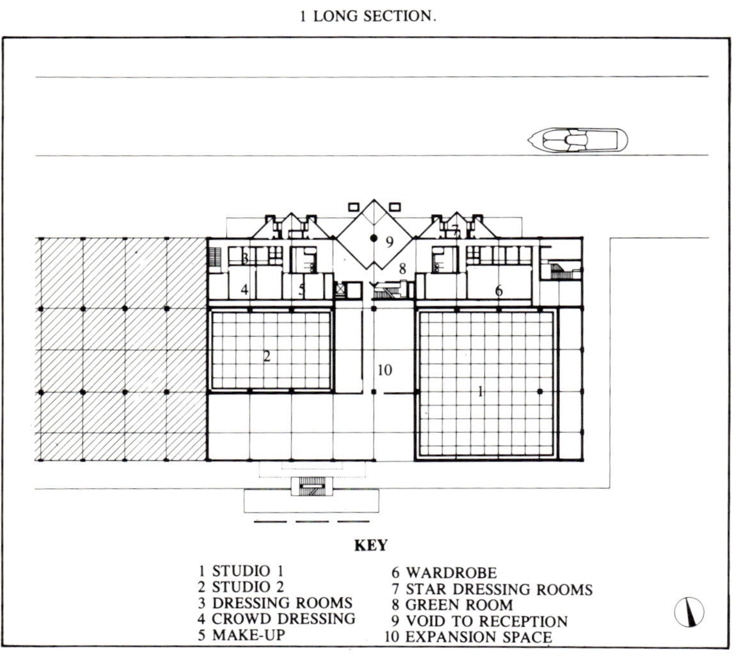

3 MEZZANINE FLOOR.

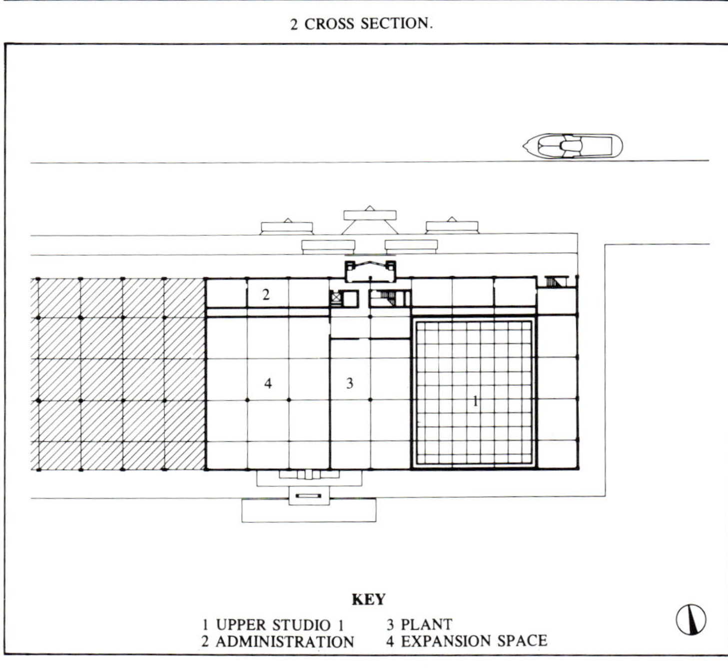

4 SECOND FLOOR.

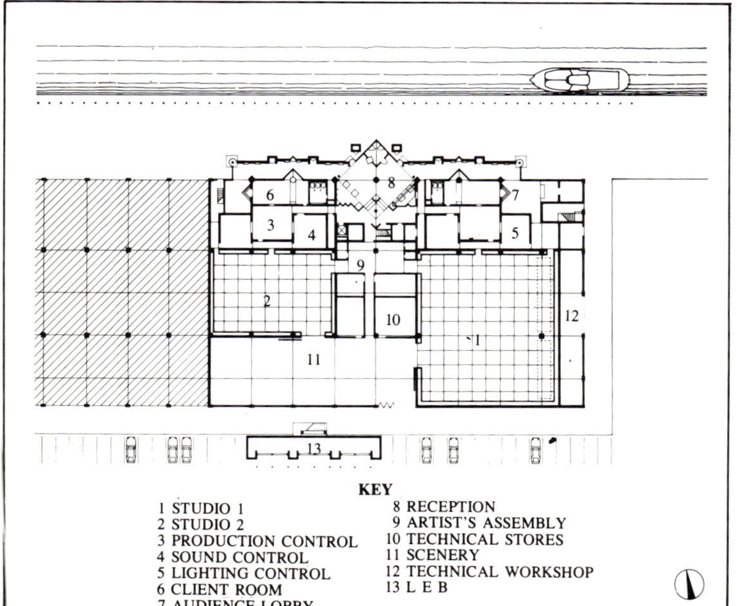

5 GROUND FLOOR.

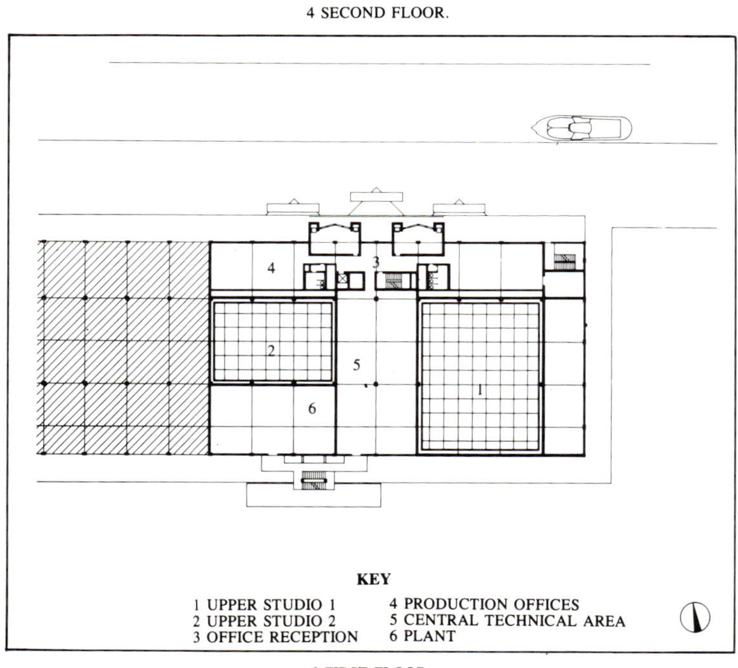

6 FIRST FLOOR.

TERRY FARRELL PARTNERSHIP
Limehouse Studios, Canary Wharf, West India Docks, London 1981-3

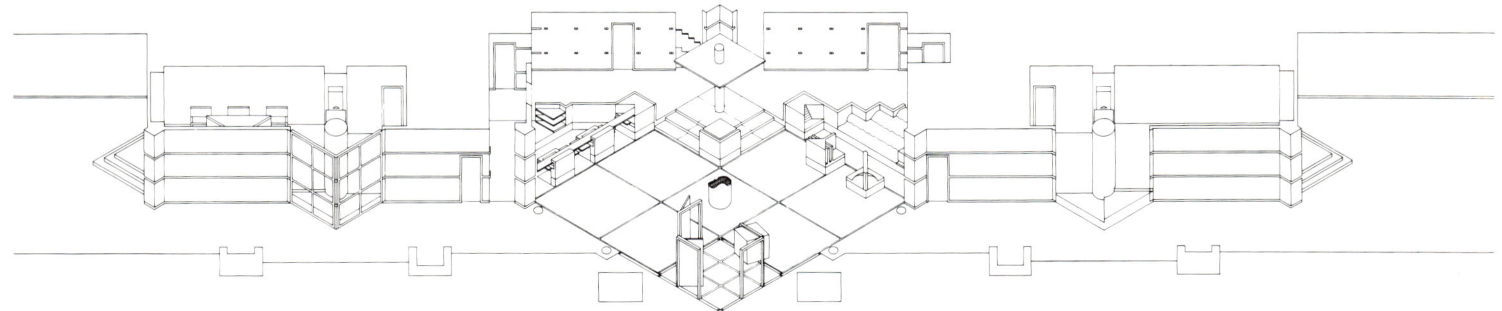

7 AXONOMETRIC.

The Terry Farrell Partnership were appointed in November 1981 to undertake a feasibility study for creating a television production and recording studio centre within the London Docklands Enterprise Zone at the Isle of Dogs.

We examined three potential new building sites and several buildings for conversion. This existing 1950s warehouse was soon identified as the best option because of its ideal location at the end of Canary Wharf, the tremendous resource value of its existing structure, and the timescale and volumetric advantages of a conversion as opposed to a purpose-built studio.

The initial proposal was to take only four to five structural bays of the existing building—into which the smaller studio and all technical, office and other back-up areas could easily be accommodated—and to build the larger studio on vacant land to the east. However, the expense involved in driving new foundations through filled rum vaults beneath Canary Wharf led us to re-examine the possibility of the major structural adaptation necessary to accommodate the larger studio within the existing building. This proved to be more economical; supporting the existing roof structure on a new system of castellated beams (which also support the independently hung inner studio box) and allowing the removal of three bays of existing structure for the entire height of the building, thus transferring all loads back onto the original adjacent piled foundations.

Once the ideal studio locations were fixed by structural considerations, the remainder of the internal planning was very flexible, many options being possible within the framework of the large existing structural grid. The basic concept finally adopted for the internal planning was for large spaces and technical and plant rooms to occupy the central and southern bays next to the new service road, whilst all client rooms, dressing rooms, production and administrative offices would be concentrated on the northern face of the building with its large cantilevered balconies overlooking the dockside and water. The large ground storey height is ideal for scenery storage and assembly, but a new mezzanine floor has been inserted over control rooms and client room to provide dressing and make-up rooms, and an artists' green room overlooking the central reception area.

The opportunity has been taken to provide a new identity for this disused warehouse, not by attempting to reface or combat the massive bulk and visual strength of the existing building, but by exploiting the 'add on' character of the new elements and the contrast they provide with the long receding lines of the existing balconies. By this means it has been possible to express the exciting new use of the building, in an economical yet forceful way. On the dockside elevation, a strong pyramidal arrangement of vitreous enamel-clad trabeated elements mark the entrance to the studios, and the principal client areas. At ground floor level, this new structure forms a continuous glazed promenade, outside the line of the existing building. This new pyramid structure is highly articulated, and strongly coloured in sympathy with the Limehouse logo.

The central entrance and rather formal symmetrical arrangement of the two studios and their respective sets of client and control rooms lead to a simply expressed circulation system which concentrates all major activity along the public face of the building. At the hub of these two major circulation axes, the main reception area is formed from a square, set at 45° to the strong lines of the existing building; this device sets up a geometry which runs right through the facade to express the entrance, star dressing rooms, and major office areas.

The remaining three sides of the building are handled in a simpler manner, disciplined by the exposed concrete framework and the rhythm of individual balconies and goods doors. The new elements of escape stairs, services intake, air conditioning louvres and scenery doors concentrate these rhythms, and are to be brightly coloured 'clip on' highly engineered elements sympathetic to the original docklands visual character and scale. However, the new roof plant, roof-mounted microwave and satellite receiving dish (currently temporarily located on the undeveloped western half) will extend this visual reference and relate to the docklands' emerging role as a centre for the new technologies of communication.

Detail design commenced in earnest in May 1982: Laing's were appointed as Management Contractors and construction started on site in October 1982. Engineering installation commenced in March 1983; the studios and control rooms were undertaken first to allow technical installation, and were completed on programme to allow trial productions to be undertaken during October, the whole building being completed in November 1983.

Plans are now well advanced for the erection in the western half of the building of smaller studios, rehearsal spaces, and various other linked facilities for Limehouse and other related users to produce a total production centre for TV unique in this country.

ARCHITECTS Terry Farrell Partnership
STRUCTURAL CONSULTANTS Broad & Gloyens
SERVICES CONSULTANTS Sandy Brown Associates, MSU
QUANTITY SURVEYORS Gleeds
ACOUSTIC CONSULTANTS Sandy Brown Associates
TECHNICAL ADVISOR Sir James Redmond
MANAGEMENT CONTRACTOR Laing Management Contracting

8-10 ENTRANCE FACADE. (PHS RICHARD BRYANT)

11, 12 VIEWS OF THE RECEPTION AREA. (PHS RICHARD BRYANT)

JAMES STIRLING, MICHAEL WILFORD & ASSOCIATES

Villa Lingotto, Turin 1984

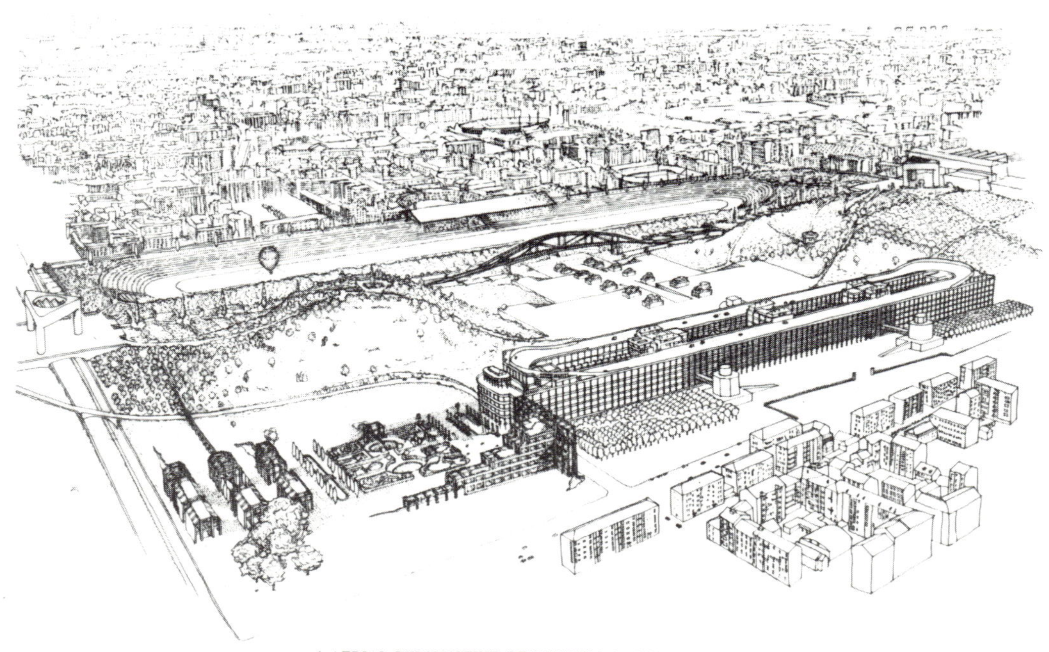

1 AERIAL PERSPECTIVE OF THE VILLA AND GARDENS.

Villa Lingotto sits in a new piazza of the same name off the lengthy and populous Via Nizza. Built for Giovanni Agnelli Sr, to Giacomo Matté Trucco's plans, its construction began in 1917 and continued to 1926. It was conceived both by architect and client as the most innovative and extensive car manufacturing plant of the time, built on a structural grid which allowed for maximum flexibility and incorporated a futuristic and much admired test track circuit on the roof.

Since 1984, the building has been devoted to the exhibition and study of Italian Industrial Design. Architects of this transformation were James Stirling, Michael Wilford Associates, the British firm practising in London.

Approaching the vast frontage, pedestrians coming from the city are directed by two ramps reaching out into the piazza to the new Entrance Pavilions which lead to the first floor of the facilities.

The fine Drive in the Museum (13,284 sq.m.) and Design School (13,284 sq.m.), both unique of their kind, are linked at each level, thus enabling visitors particularly interested in the process of design as well as in the final product to take a look at the workshops or attend lectures and seminars.

For those arriving by car, whether by Autostrada or from the centre of Turin, ample parking facilities for 2,165 car spaces are provided in the two end sections of the building. Access to the Museum and School occurs directly from each floor of the carpark.

To the left of the Villa is the celebrated Water Garden, a romantic industrial ruin evoking memories of the illustrious Press Centre which once stood on this site. Shaded pools. formal parterres, labyrinths and nymphaea enhance this quiet secluded garden.

Having concluded the tour of the Museum and Water Garden, it is recommended that visitors should find their way back to the Piazza and then proceed under the colonnade, through the ramped courts, to the Terrazza Grande which offers a breathtaking view of the Villa's grounds.

A Stone Arena for cycling, ballooning and horse racing crowns the vista to the west, before the background of the snow-capped Alps. A series of stepping terraces (in the manner of Versailles), flanked by highly polished marble Car Sphinxes lead to the intersection of the Viale Centrale with the Salita Lunga, where dramatic upward views are offered unexpectedly, both towards the Stazione Novissima (1985) to the north and towards the functional yet pleasing Paracheggio della Torre (1985) which concludes the Autostrada.

Conversely, travellers by train into Turin will get an exciting fleeting glimpse of the Villa and gardens as they briefly emerge from the tunnel onto the humped bridge on axis with the Villa itself, before being re-engulfed into the ground.

Triangular Gates fronting the station and carpark somewhat reminiscent of Guarino Guarini boldly step over the roads which create the boundaries of the Villa's gardens, emphasising the side entrances to the park.

Returning to the Villa, one climbs the great Earth Mounds, a true feat of sculptural landscaping, providing relief from the relentless quality of 500 metres of concrete and glass facade.

Refreshments are available both in the Ristorante Il Triangolo and at the Bar Agnelli, the latter located on the Piazza level.

Having regained your vehicle, depart via the famous Roof Track still the symbol of the Villa, indulge in a quick spin before returning down the highly expressionist ramps (originally built in 1927-8 and now freed of their outer walls) to the starting point of your next excursion.

ARCHITECTS James Stirling, Michael Wilford & Associates with Robert Portchmouth, Barbara Weiss, Robert Dye, Christopher McCormack

2 TRANSVERSE SECTION ACROSS THE VILLA AND GARDENS.

3 PERSPECTIVE ON THE PIAZZA.

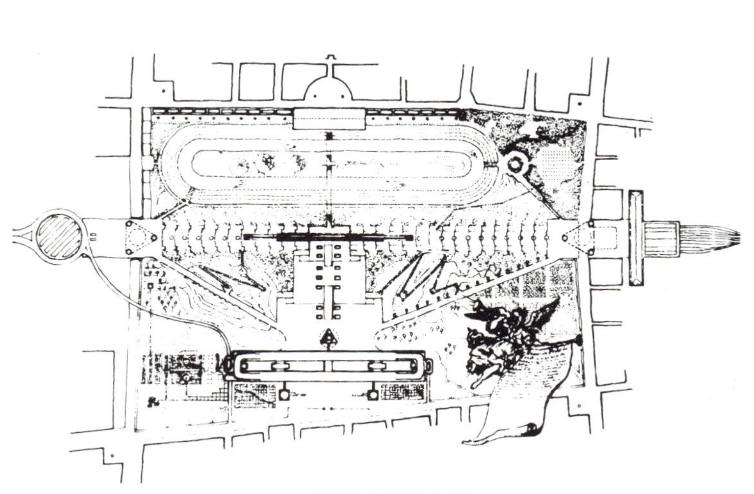

4 GENERAL SITE PLAN.

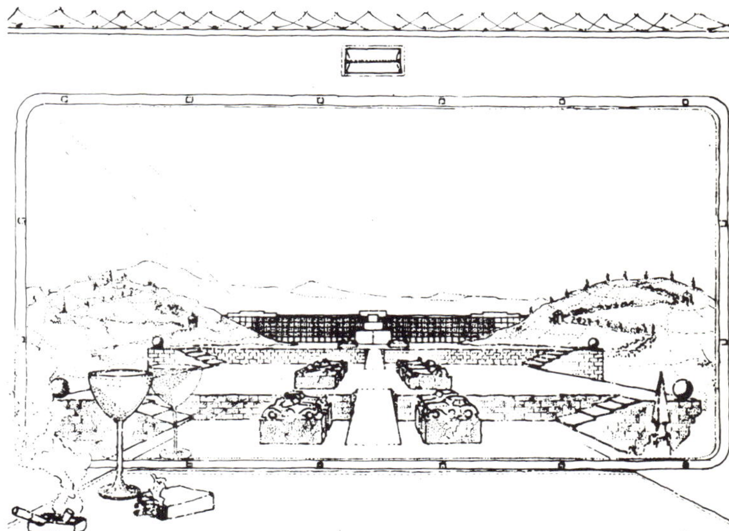

5 VIEW FROM THE TRAIN.

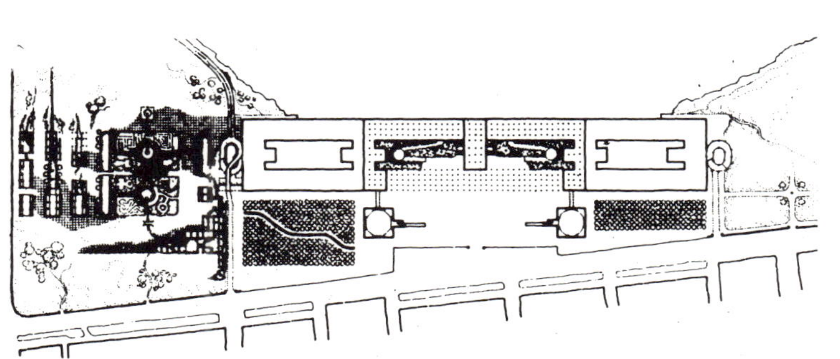

6 PIAZZA LEVEL PLAN.

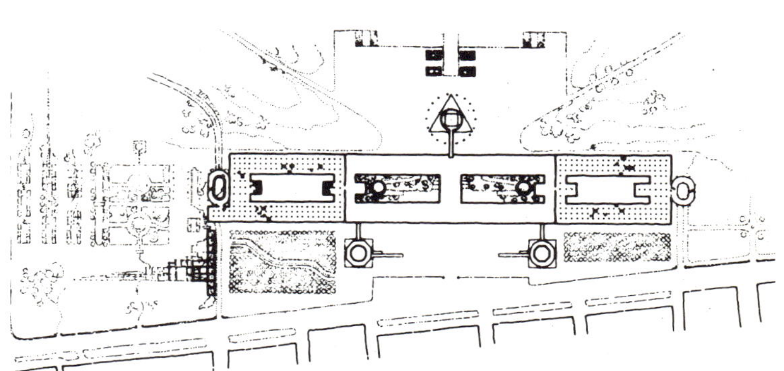

7 PLAN OF DRIVE-IN PARKING.

8 PERSPECTIVE OF THE GARDENS.

RICHARD ROGERS + PARTNERS
Whittington Avenue, City of London, 1982–3

In September 1982 Richard Rogers + Partners were appointed by Speyhawk PLC to prepare a scheme for the comprehensive development of the sites, on both sides of Whittington Avenue in the City of London. Speyhawk PLC had previously worked jointly with Richard Rogers + Partners on the Hampton Site Competition for the National Gallery Extension. The sites at Whittington Avenue are primarily City Corporation freehold properties with the principal longer-term leasehold interests held at that time by Speyhawk. However, a single smaller building on the Gracechurch Street frontage was in the freehold ownership of the Dominion Insurance Company.

The Clients' Brief

1 The acceptable plot ratio for the site is 5:1.
2 Approximately 150,000 sq ft net of lettable office/trading space, 50% deep plan, 50% shallow plan. The trading space to be planned at the lower levels to accommodate financial markets and similar activities.
3 Shopping facilities at lower ground, ground and first floor levels to integrate with the existing market activity in the Leadenhall Market adjacent.
4 A City library of approximately 8,000 sq ft of net usable space.
5 The pedestrian routes should relate through to the new Lloyd's development adjacent.

Site Investigation

1 Initial site investigations clearly identified the importance of the Leadenhall Street/Gracechurch Street corner and the necessity to maintain the visual line along the Leadenhall Street frontage through to the corner of Whittington Avenue.
2 Pedestrian activity in the market should clearly be extended through the site along narrow covered routes.
3 The present vehicular servicing arrangement to the market along the narrow covered streets is clearly unhealthy and in conflict with pedestrian activity. Methods of catering for market servicing traffic on the site were investigated.
4 The future road widening intentions along Gracechurch Street have to be respected.

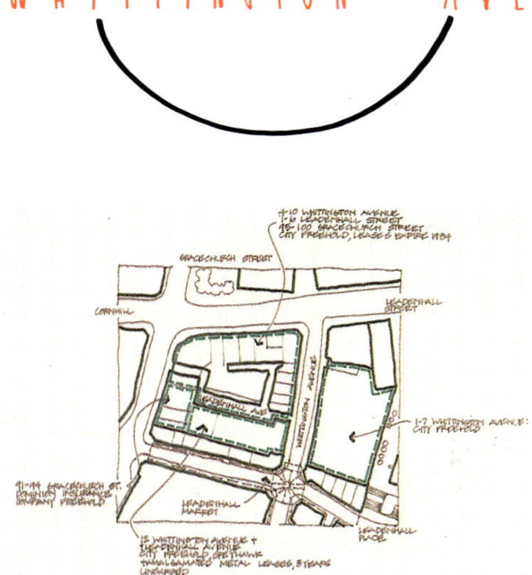

2 SITE OWNERSHIP DIAGRAM.

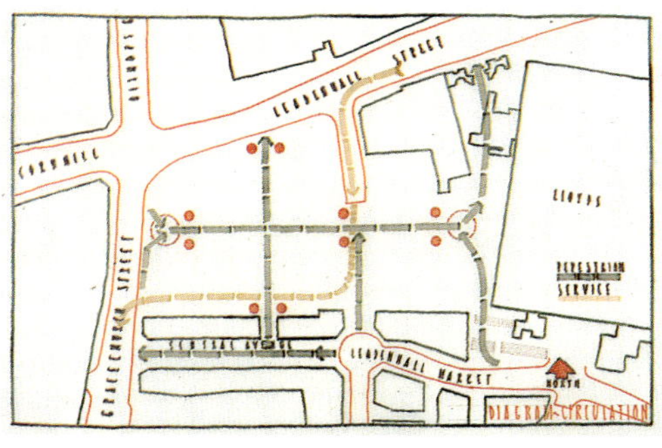

3 PEDESTRIAN/VEHICULAR SERVICING DIAGRAM.

Comprehensive Scheme Design

1 The building is formed by a series of large overlapping spaces integrated around a central escalator-way which bisects the site, dividing the building diagonally into two parts. The part below is potentially deep plan whilst the part above could be let as small shallow plan offices. The escalator linking all the floors extends the pavement outside to the top of the building. Galleries in the air run either side of the escalator-way and offer access to the spaces either side. These galleries in effect offer high level 'street frontage' to all levels, thus offering great flexibility in the division of space and enhancing the letting potential.
2 Ground level restaurant facilities and entrances to the lower level trading floors push out to the pavement edge at the Whittington Avenue crossing, thus celebrating the secondary access to Leadenhall

RESPONSE TO THE CLIENT'S BRIEF
COMPREHENSIVE DEVELOPMENT FOR BOTH SIDES OF WHITTINGTON AVENUE ADJACENT TO LLOYD'S

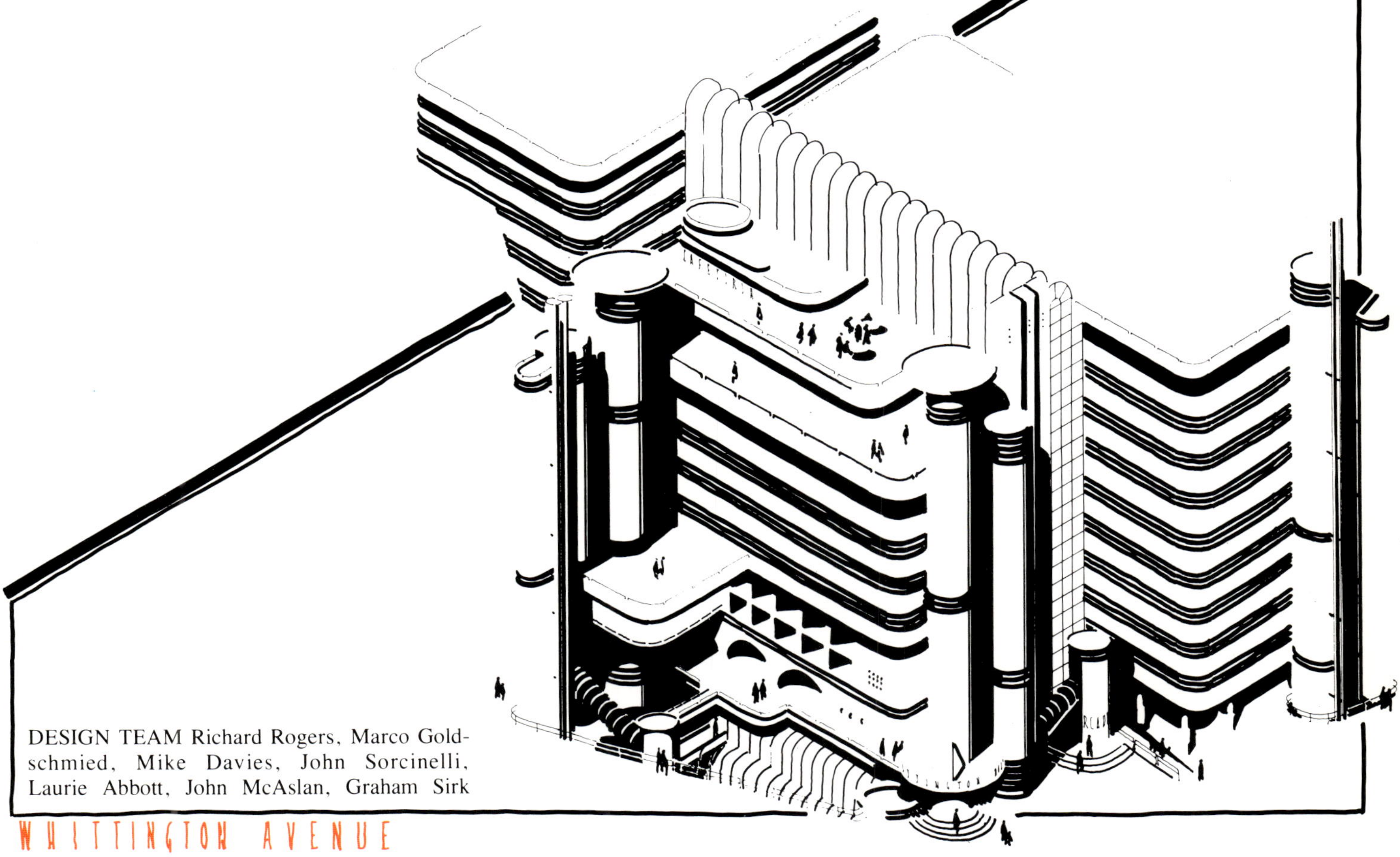

DESIGN TEAM Richard Rogers, Marco Goldschmied, Mike Davies, John Sorcinelli, Laurie Abbott, John McAslan, Graham Sirk

WHITTINGTON AVENUE

Market and retaining the visual line along Leadenhall Street. The escalator-way flies over Whittington Avenue at high level.

3 Large open and deep plan trading floors are designed for the lower levels for use by banks and financial market users.

4 Principal entrance facilities are concentrated on the Leadenhall/Gracechurch Street corner thus opening the scheme to this visually significant urban intersection.

5 The principle east/west axis of the escalator-way is focused on the east facade of St Peter Cornhill, one of the oldest landmarks in the City of London.

6 Existing servicing traffic along the Central Avenue of the Leadenhall Market is to be diverted to a servicing yard on the site, thus helping to alleviate the present pedestrian traffic conflict.

7 Controlled access entrance facilities were investigated from the present Lloyd's site adjacent on the east.

8 Pedestrian routes at ground level are designed to help tie the Leadenhall Market activities through to Leadenhall Street and the Lloyd's development.

Discussions with the City Planners

After being presented with the initial sketch concepts in October 1982 the City Architect and Planning Officers opposed the idea of a comprehensive solution. It was eventually decided by the City Corporation that the City Officers would prepare a brief. The brief was distributed in late March the following year, approximately 6 months after design work commenced.

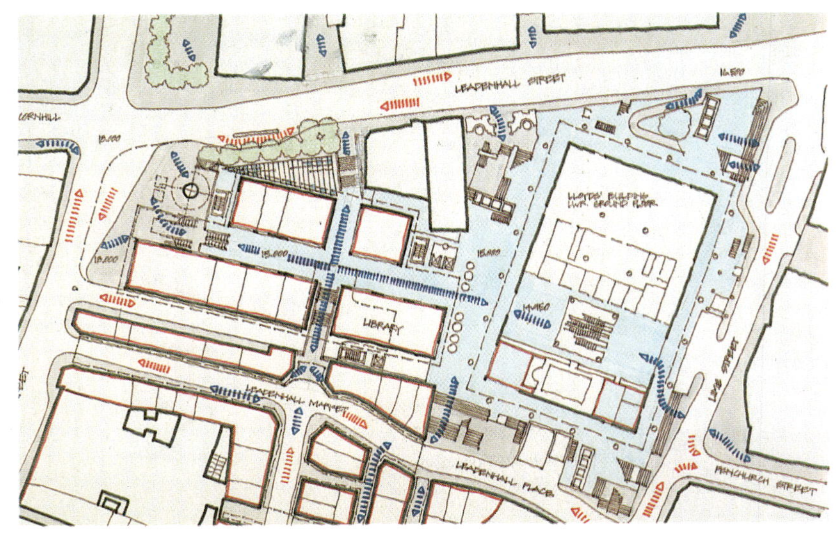

5 PEDESTRIAN/VEHICULAR CIRCULATION AT GROUND/LWR GROUND (PROPOSAL).

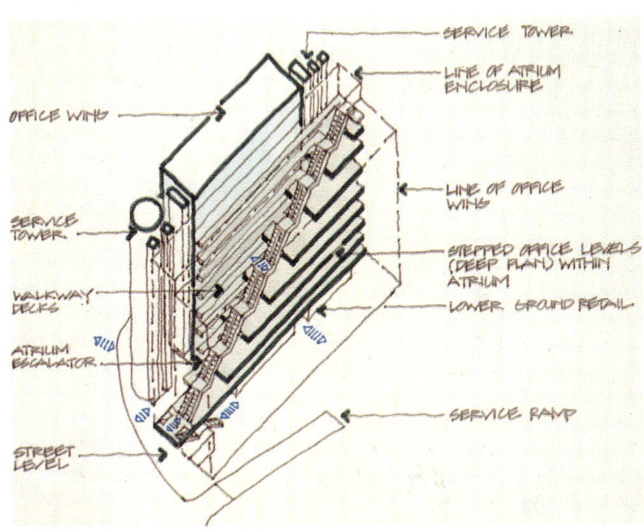

6 DIAGRAMMATIC CUTAWAY AXONOMETRIC.

RESPONSE TO THE CLIENT'S BRIEF

SITE FOLLOWING DEVELOPMENT FOR THE SITE WEST OF WHITTINGTON AVENUE

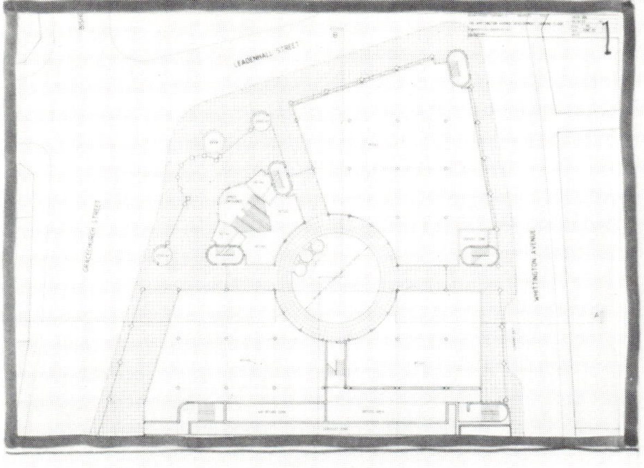

7 GROUND PLAN (1).

8-10 MASSING & ELEVATIONAL STUDIES (2-4).

Scheme 2

The client, though in disagreement with the City's position, instructed Richard Rogers + Partners to prepare a scheme for the site west of Whittington Avenue and to try and satisfy the City's requirements. Richard Rogers + Partners undertook design studies, the intentions of which were as follows:

Design Intentions in Response to the City Brief

1 The spaces are grouped around a circular public courtyard, daylit from above. The public space links the existing pedestrian routes with entrances focused on the principle view of St Peter Cornhill and the primary vista up Bishopsgate.

2 The building conforms to the site boundary on all sides except on the Gracechurch Street frontage where it conforms to the new road widening line. A pedestrian arcade along this Gracechurch Street frontage conforms to the requirements of the City's Brief.

3 The corner entrance is celebrated and provides a focus for views down Bishopsgate from the north and along Cornhill from the west.

4 Provisions for a services yard for the shops along the Central Avenue of Leadenhall Market were proposed, thus allowing the pedestrianisation of this historic City market street.

11 URBAN MASSING & SKYLINE STUDY.

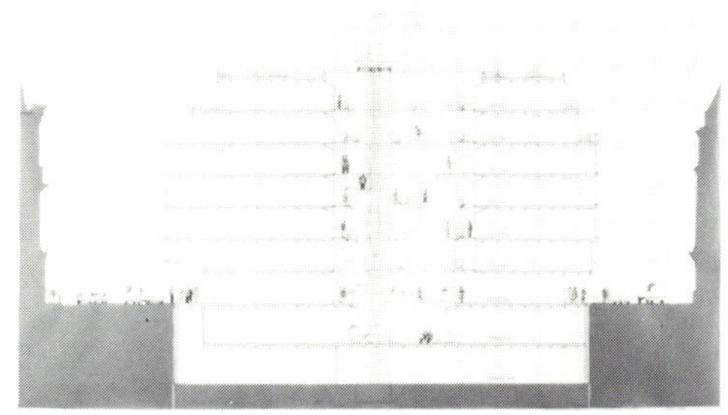

12 CROSS SECTION THROUGH CENTRAL SPACE.

13 CURRENT SERVICING ARRANGEMENTS TO LEADENHALL MARKET WITH THE OBVIOUS PEDESTRIAN CONFLICT.

14 PROPOSED PEDESTRIANISATION OF CENTRAL AVENUE, LEADENHALL MARKET.

15 INITIAL PROPOSAL FOR GROUND PLAN WITH SERVICING YARD FOR LEADENHALL MARKET, THUS CENTRAL MARKET AVENUE IS PEDESTRIANISED.

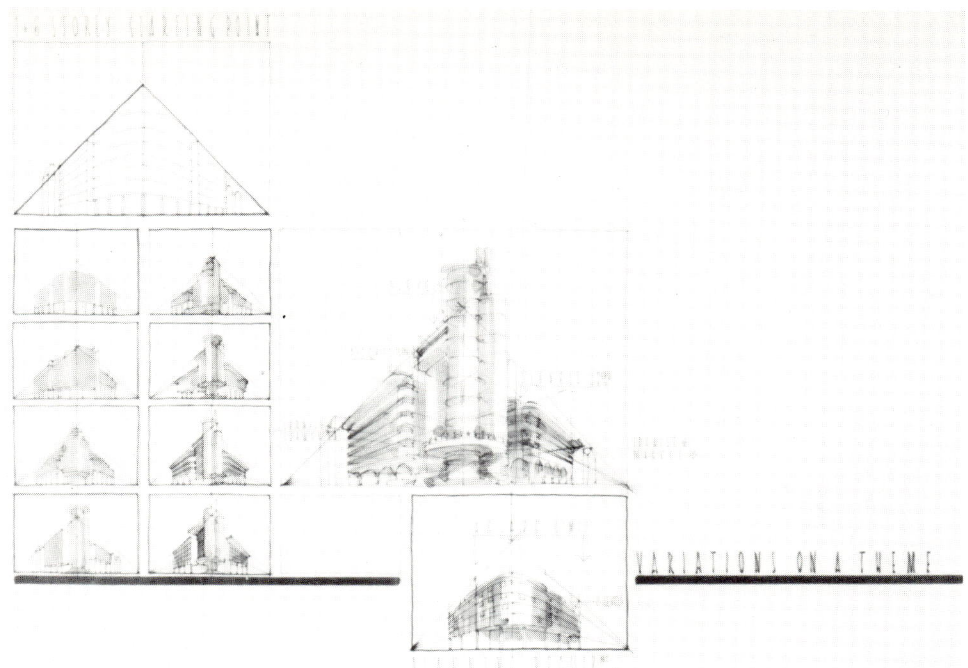

RESPONSE TO THE CITY ARCHITECT'S ELEVATIONAL CRITERIA

Richard Rogers + Partners met with the City Architect and Planning Officers over the design for the site west of Whittington Avenue. From those meetings the following drawings were developed to conform to the City Architect's design criteria. The following opinions were expressed by the City Architect and Planning Officers at those meetings:

1 The new development should conform to the existing building envelope except for the frontage along Gracechurch Street which must conform to the new road widening line.

2 The facade of the new building should be Victorian in character.

3 The facade should be heavy, ideally made of stone.

4 The corner should be solid and treated in a similarly heavy way. A xerox copy of a Victorian Glasgow building was presented to Richard Rogers + Partners by the Planners as an appropriate corner and facade solution.

5 No account should be taken of the nearby existing modern buildings as this architecture is now out of favour.

6 Double height pedestrian arcade must extend along the Gracechurch Street frontage. This arcade should not extend around the corner on to the Leadenhall frontage.

7 Circular stone arches should be designed for the Gracechurch Street arcade. The City preferred solid arches to more carved and open arches and suggested faience angles would be appropriate decorative elements for the quoins.

8 No need to extend the public zone at street level. The existing pedestrian route through the site is private and should remain so.

9 No attempt should be made to pedestrianise the Leadenhall Market. (Because of the high level of lead pollution due to the traffic using the covered market streets, the market shops will be required to be glazed in the near future). The City Planners prefer the current arrangements despite existing difficulties.

17 EXAMPLE OF SUGGESTED FACADE & CORNER TREATMENT.

Concluding Satement

The City Architect and Planning Officers were encouraged by the designs prepared in accordance with their instructions, but the client felt as follows about the approach: 'The original intention to develop a modern building suited to the present day needs of banking and commerce were clearly contrary to the stated preference of the City Architect and Planning Officers for a more traditional design solution. The difficulty experienced in obtaining consent for a scheme fulfilling the requirements of the initial brief together with the apparent acceptance of alternative and more traditional approaches to design led the company to abandon its plans and to dispose of its interest in the site to an institution holding other leases on the site and who now propose to proceed with an alternative development scheme.'

Trevor Osborne,
Chairman & Joint Managing Director
Speyhawk Land & Estates Limited

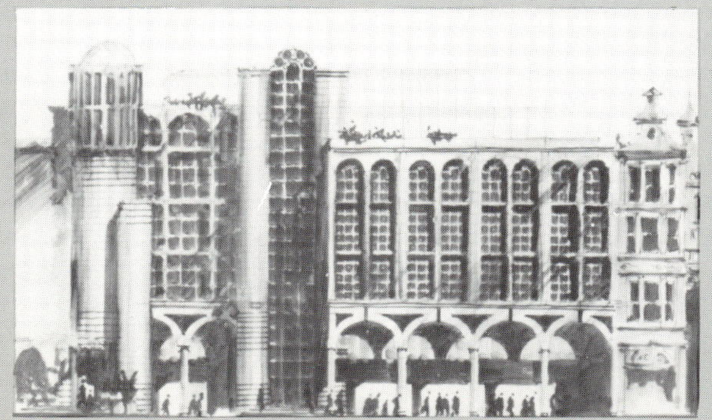

18 ELEVATIONAL STUDY, GRACECHURCH STREET, PREPARED IN ACCORDANCE WITH THE DESIGN GUIDANCE GIVEN BY THE CITY ARCHITECT'S DEPARTMENT.

19 ELEVATIONAL STUDY, GRACECHURCH STREET, PREPARED IN ACCORDANCE WITH THE DESIGN GUIDANCE GIVEN BY THE CITY ARCHITECT'S DEPARTMENT.

Progress

The new Headquarters for the Hong Kong and Shanghai Banking Corporation is now at an advanced stage of construction. The steel frame has practically reached its 180m height. Cladding of the structure and the external walls has progressed from street level to about one third of the height of the building. Major central services plant installation is proceeding in the basement, whilst the pre-assembled floor based service modules and risers are being swung into position on the steelwork. Complex service distribution within the suspended floors is developing. Pre-assembled escalators and lift components are being fitted sequentially as the building becomes enclosed. Off site preparations and manufacture of special internal fit-out systems and components is continuing. First occupation is planned for mid 1985.

Services Modules

The services modules develop the technology of prefabrication—from initial sketches prepared by the architects, structural engineers and services engineers a 1:50 model was constructed. From this a full size timber mock-up was made, to check layout of components. Next a full working prototype was built: this was used for approvals of details and finishes, but also provided vital performance checks for air-conditioning capacity, noise levels, vibration and structural weight. Fabrication of the production modules was carried out on an assembly line in Japan and after fitting external protection the units were shipped to Hong Kong and transported to site by low loading road trailors. All units were delivered and hoisted by night, at the rate of two in each 24 hour period. Once in position the modules remain locked, to avoid wear and tear or accidental internal damage prior to commissioning.

See also *AD* 51 3/4-1981 'British Architects', pp 18-27.

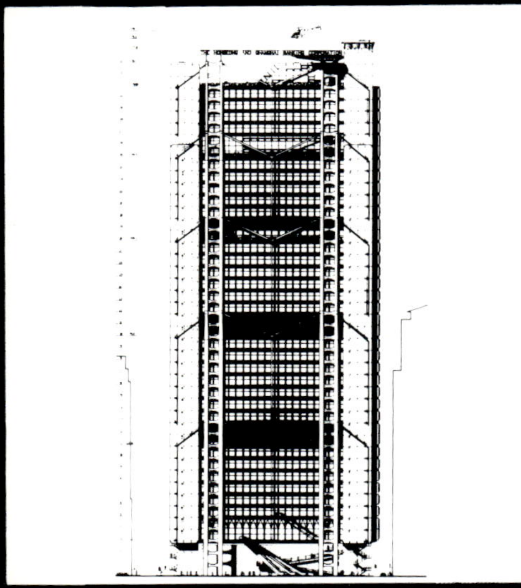

1 HARBOURSIDE ELEVATION.

ARCHITECTS Foster Associates Hong Kong
STRUCTURAL AND CIVIL ENGINEERS
Ove Arup and Partners Hong Kong Ltd
SERVICES CONSULTING ENGINEERS
J Roger Preston (Central) Ltd
QUANTITY SURVEYORS Levett and Bailey
JOINT MANAGEMENT CONTRACTORS
John Lok/Wimpey

2 EVENING VIEW OF THE SOUTH SIDE OF THE BUILDING FROM THE PEAK. (PH JOHN NYE)

NORMAN FOSTER ASSOCIATES
Hongkong and Shanghai Banking Corporation Headquarters, 1979, 1982–5

EL WAKIL ASSOCIATES
The Island Mosque, Corniche, Jeddah, Saudi Arabia 1983-4

1984 AWARDS

1 EAST ELEVATION.

Modern architecture and western technology have been an integral part of Saudi Arabia's economic boom. The vast amount of building that has taken place in recent years has been regarded as evidence of progress regardless of whether it was good or bad. This desire for progress has overshadowed architecture's crucial function as a profound expression of man's existence on earth and the preservation of his identity. Instead of creating an 'ideal environment through the visible expression of organised space', recent mosques have been functional buildings for the accommodation of worshippers with a few surface embellishments. There is a need for sacred architecture to be restored as an expression of the spiritual through an ideal location to serve man at the moment of worship and meditation. This has been the objective of The Mayor of Jeddah and architect Mohammed Said Farsi in collaboration with Sheikh Hossam Khashoggi, Deputy Minister of Pilgrimage and Endowment.

A site was selected in Jeddah and the plans for a small mosque (*masjid*) chosen as a prototype of Islamic architectural design which related to the historical situation and cultural traditions. A position was chosen possessing 'spirit of place', isolated, so as to have maximum visual impact. A small island was created on the edge of a coral reef just off the new corniche, to the north of Jeddah. The approach was designed to meander along the shore leading to a narrow bridge, in order to 'gather the landscape into a certain location' and so uncover its value as a symbol. The path which leads to the sacred place crosses over water and thus becomes a symbolic journey of pilgrimage.

Having defined the position, the symbolic meaning of the various parts of the building needed delineating as part of a religious architectural language. Words, like the forms they describe, must be realised in their true meaning: so 'original' does not mean novel or different but a return to the origin of things; 'creative' refers back to the Creator, Architect of the universe. Likewise, the concept of design is based on the prototype of forms. The principle of 'Squaring the Circle' represents the relationship of the dome (sphere) to the prayer hall (cube): the sphere stands for the circular, the heavenly; the cube for the solid, the earthbound. In the same way, the vertical is qualitative representing man's aspirations, while the horizontal is quantitative implying the concrete world of action.

In this building the dome leads the eye upwards, accentuating vertical direction by hollowing out space. In addition, it has been placed directly over the *mihrab* (prayer niche) though slightly off-centre, thus emphasising by lateral displacement its directions towards Makkah.

The prayer hall has a huge arched opening on the west side. Inside are two pillars, thick masonry walls, deep rebates—all bathed in light filtered from above. It is approached through a paved courtyard providing a centre to the mosque which is emphasised by geometric paving patterns. The courtyard provides a horizontal outlook through reoccuring arches to the sea where heaven and earth are fused visually and physically at the horizon. It is entered by means of a 'bent' entrance which leads to a doorway under the minaret and provides a demarcation between the outside and inside.

Even though the voice of the muezzin has been replaced by loudspeakers, the minaret remains a potent architectural symbol. Its vertical element expresses the dimension of space and man's yearning towards the skies. Inside, the staircase leads up to a square balcony topped by a dome on a cube; *muqarnas* (stalactites) embellish the balcony, adding to the vision of an elegant flower reaching heavenwards. Like a spiritual lighthouse it stands as a beacon, magnet of the spirit.

All of these architectural elements are brought together in the mosque to express the universal in terms of the man-made. Myth, symbol and nature are encased in geometric proportion to convey an ideal vision of the Divine. The architect has used the basic pattern structures of the universe as his tools to create a building that inspires awe and humility.

ARCHITECTS A W El Wakil & Associates
CLIENT Ministry of Pilgrimage and Endowment with the municipality of Jeddah
LANDSCAPE DESIGN Rik Sturdy Associates
WATERCOLOUR PRESENTATIONS E Venn

2 WEST ELEVATION.

3 EAST-WEST SECTION.

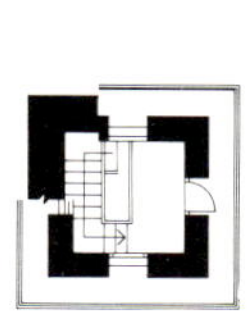

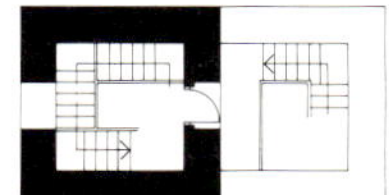

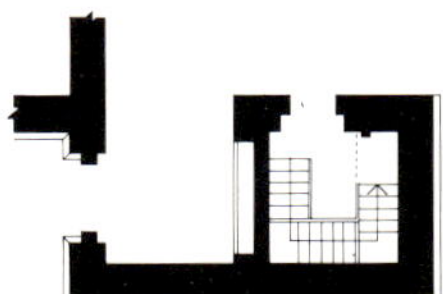

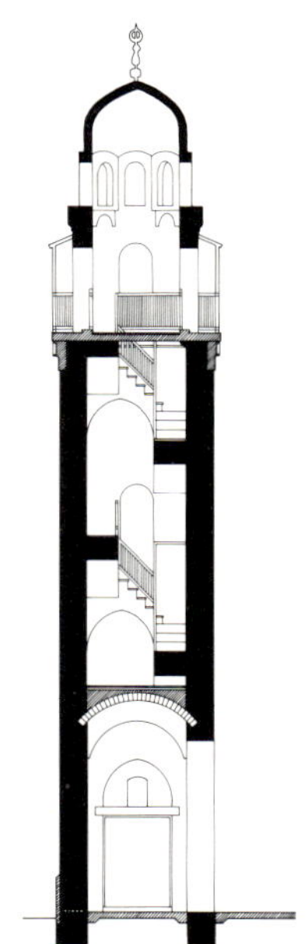

4-6 PLANS AND VERTICAL SECTIONS OF MINARET.

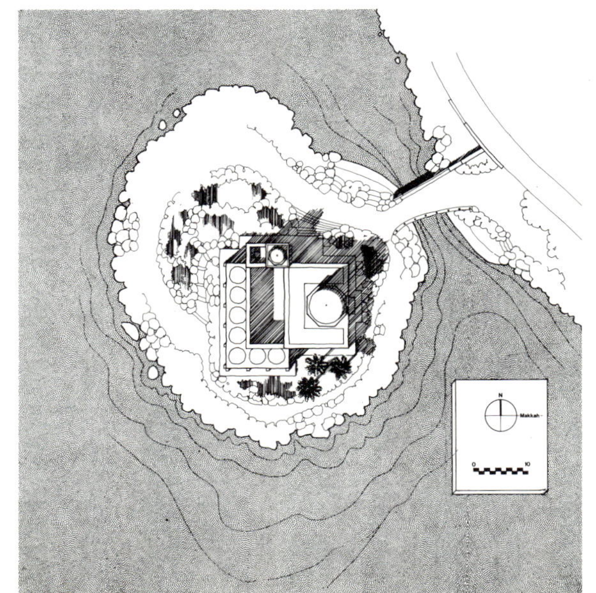

7 SITE PLAN.

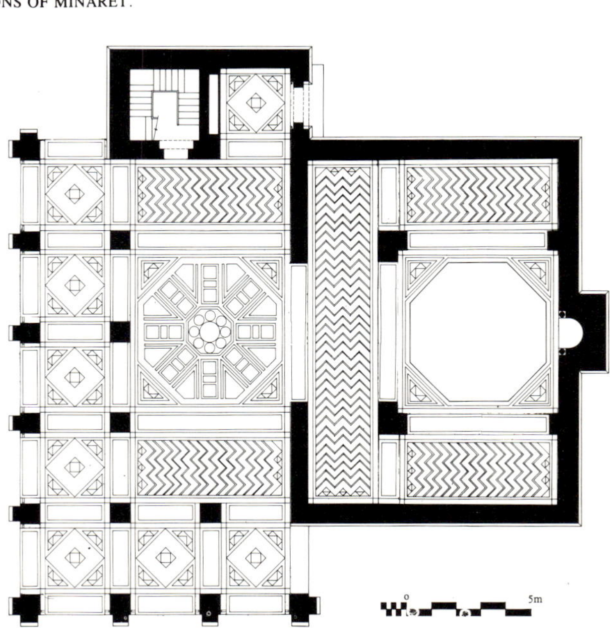

8 GROUND FLOOR PLAN.

9 AERIAL VIEW OF MODEL.

10, 11 VIEWS OF DOMES UNDER CONSTRUCTION.